weekend sewer's guide to
Blouses

weekend sewer's guide to

Blouses

TIME-SAVING SEWING WITH A CREATIVE TOUCH

Kate Mathews

LARK
BOOKS

Art Director: Dana Irwin

Photography: Evan Bracken

Illustrations: Pete Adams, Lisa Mandle, Bernadette Wolf

Production: Dana Irwin

Editorial Assistance: Val Anderson

Library of Congress Cataloging-in-Publication Data

Mathews, Kate.

     The weekend sewer's guide to blouses : time-saving sewing with a creative touch / Kate Mathews.

p. cm.

     "A Lark sewing book."

     Includes index.

     ISBN 1-57990-032-1

1. Blouses. 2. Machine sewing.   I. Title.

TT545.M37   1998

646.4'35-dc21   97-43021

                            CIP

10 9 8 7 6 5 4 3 2 1

First Edition

Published by Lark Books

50 College St.

Asheville, NC 28801, US

© 1998, Lark Books

Distributed by Random House, Inc., in the United States, Canada, the United Kingdom, Europe, and Asia

Distributed in Australia by Capricorn Link (Australia) Pty Ltd., P.O. Box 6651, Baulkham Hills Business Centre, NSW 2153, Australia

Distributed in New Zealand by Tandem Press Ltd., 2 Rugby Rd., Birkenhead, Auckland, New Zealand

CONTENTS

A blouse is the most basic building block of any wardrobe. It's often the first garment we ever make in a sewing or home economics class, and probably the garment we make most often. We depend on it to go with everything, from skirts and pants to jumpers and jackets. A blouse can be worn under other garments, over them, or by itself. It can be tailored or frilly, stripped down and basic, or dramatic art-to-wear. In any case, once you've passed up the dresses hanging in your closet, you will have to reach for a blouse—or go naked.

After several years of sewing blouses, it's easy to get bored with the basic pattern styles. Just look in your closet—there are probably several versions of your favorite patterns hanging in a row. Camp shirt, jewel-neck pullover, T-shirt, classic button-front long-sleeved blouse, roomy tunic, and perhaps one or two unusual styles, such as a Japanese-inspired asymmetrical front or kimono wrap blouse. Some of them fit perfectly and you feel great when you wear them, but others are kind of humdrum and do nothing for your spirit when you put them on. But one thing's for sure: when you're strolling the aisles of your favorite fabric store and your hands light on some fabulous material, you'll see one of those blouse patterns in your mind's eye, made up in the fabric at hand.

THE BASIC
WHITE BLOUSE
IS SUCH A
CLASSIC—IT
GOES WITH
EVERYTHING!

Because a blouse typically is one component of an outfit, rather than a stand-alone garment, it has to be a stylish piece on its own and also complement its ensemble companions without overwhelming them. You can pull out all the design stops on a dress, but a blouse has to be a kind of chameleon,

CREATIVITY. WHICH
OFTEN SEEMS TO
REQUIRE EXTRA
TIME. CAN ACTUALLY
BE THE MOST
EFFECTIVE
TIME-SAVER.

able to look beautiful with a number of other garments. This is why the basic white blouse is such a classic—it goes with everything!

As a sewer, though, making up another white blouse can seem kind of boring and therefore dampen your sewing enthusiasm. You probably don't sew to turn out identical gar-

ments one after the other. You can always go to the store and buy another white shirt. Instead, you sew to inspire yourself, enjoy the process of working with cloth, and create wearables that are original, versatile, and truly individual.

A perfect occasion may be coming up soon and you don't have the time to refine a brand new pattern, so you'll pull out an old standby that fits well and assembles quickly. But this time, you wonder just how to make it up again, varying it with a differ-

ent twist or some unique styling. That's where this book comes in—to help you refresh your creative stores of energy and apply a special touch to the dependable pattern, for a brand new blouse that you can also get done in time to wear to that special event.

Creativity, which often seems to require extra time, can actually be the most effective time-saver. A simple yet creative innovation may take far less time in the long run than shopping for an unusual new pattern, experimenting with it to work out the kinks, and finally making it up in a selected fabric. At the same time, a special touch can add just the right pizzazz to a blouse, without making such a bold statement that it overwhelms or competes with its companion garments. The best ideas are often those that are stripped down to the simplest

GET THE MOST
OUT OF A
MIX-AND-MATCH
APPROACH TO
DRESSING

basics, such as a surprising coupling of details or a fresh presentation of traditional technique.

Just read the tips in the pages that follow and study the blouses in the photographs, to see what other designers just like you have done to keep themselves excited about sewing and to jazz up the blouse styles in their closets. You will surely come up with a whole new assortment of good ideas that are simple and quick to do, and that will refresh the most basic of pattern styles. With a selection of variations to choose from, you won't feel like you're wearing the same blouse day after day and you will get the most out of a mix-and-match approach to dressing, resulting in a fascinating wardrobe of beautifully coordinated garments. You will soon discover that good ideas stimulate even better ones, to help you get ever more design mileage out of the limited time you have to sew.

GET READY
GET SET

SEW!

GET READY...

With a Good Ide

The fuel that keeps sewers busily stitching at the machine is creativity. When the ideas are flowing, encouraging you to try something altogether new or simply make new combinations of classic elements, the sewing machine keeps humming along and the motivation to sew remains strong. But when you're in a hurry or you've got a deadline to make, such as a special occasion coming up in a week, it's an enormous challenge to dredge up another good idea. In fact, coming up with creative sewing ideas sometimes seems to take forever. Instead, you might continue making the pattern over and over without any special creative touch, just to get the garment finished.

Blouses are the wallflower cousin of the dazzling dress. Unless you go the extra mile to make them stand out, they hide behind jackets, disappear under sweaters, or get covered up with jewelry and scarves. You have to work harder and be even more innovative to make a blouse stand alone as a work of sewing art or contribute its own drama to a coordinated outfit. Additionally, achieving an extraordinary blouse style that won't overpower or compete with its companion garments requires an extra measure of creativity. Again, you might just reach for your favorite shirt pattern and turn it out one more time, as is.

On the other hand, you may have so many ideas for creative variations of that favorite pattern, you don't know what to do with them. They just keep coming—while you're sewing, sleeping, exercising, cooking, waiting for an appointment, or driving. If you're lucky enough to have more ideas than you have time to sew them up, count your blessings. And don't forget to write them down somewhere, just in case you should ever have a dry period.

Most of us are stuck with the opposite problem, of trying to come up with a truly original idea that's as spectacular as the fabric we're fondling or the pattern we've just fallen in love with. It's so easy to sew up the pattern as is, with no added attractions. But, somehow, we feel that either the fabric we're spending our precious dollars on deserves something extra or our tried-and-true no-fail pattern is entitled to a noticeably distinctive touch that will make the garment exceptional this time around.

Take the most classic of styles—the white blouse. We have worn this garment for school pictures, job interviews, important meetings, and other occasions requiring a basic, non-controversial impression. The white blouse functions as the ultimate wardrobe building block, because it goes with absolutely anything and everything. It's the foundation for vests, sweaters, jackets, and accessories. Without our creative intervention, the white blouse is so basic that it becomes invisible and never makes a fashion statement of its own.

Many times we want this invisible effect, if the star of a selected outfit is an art-to-wear necklace or a one-of-a-kind leather vest. But there are times when we don't want to cover up this basic building block. Perhaps the weather is too hot to be comfortable in a layered blouse and jacket getup or you don't have time to search the scarf drawer for the perfect complement. At these times, it sure would be nice to pull out a white blouse that has a touch of its own pizzazz, without any other accessories. All it takes to create such a main attraction is the basic fuel for your sewing energy—a good idea.

THE SEARCH FOR IDEAS

Learning to develop innovative ideas and stimulating your own creative resources doesn't mean you have to take a drawing class or study with a mentor. In fact, developing sewing design ideas doesn't take any extra time at all. It's easy to do, lots of fun, and you can fit it into your daily

LISA MANDLE, DESIGNER OF ONLY ONE ORIGINALS, HARMONIZES VINTAGE FABRICS WITH GORGEOUS TRIMS AND BUTTONS FROM HER EXTENSIVE COLLECTION TO CREATE ARTFUL FASHIONS THAT ARE SUMPTUOUS IN THEIR DETAILS. EDGINGS, APPLIQUÉ SHAPES, LAYERED FABRIC EFFECTS, AND COLLARS ASSEMBLED LIKE SCULPTURES ALL CONTRIBUTE TO THE LUXURIOUS QUALITY OF THE FINISHED PIECE. THE BASIC SILHOUETTE OF THIS "MEMORY SHIRT" MAY BE SIMPLE, BUT THE DETAILS MAKE IT SPECTACULAR.

AT LEFT IS A BEAUTIFUL EXAMPLE OF COMBINING FABRIC DESIGN WITH GARMENT STYLE TO CREATE A SINGULAR FASHION. DESIGNER M. LUANNE CARSON HAD A LOT OF FUN IN THE PROCESS, EXPERIMENTING WITH DIFFERENT ARRANGEMENTS SUGGESTED BY THE FABRIC. WHEN CUTTING OUT THE GORES OF THE SKIRT, SHE FLIPPED THE FABRIC, TO CREATE A CHEVRON EFFECT WHEN SEWN TOGETHER. THE CHEVRONS ARE ECHOED IN THE DIRECTIONAL LAYOUT OF THE BLOUSE CONSTRUCTION, AND ACCENTED BY THE CONTRASTING BIAS EDGING.

ABOVE, SIMPLE COLOR BLOCKING CAN ALTER THE APPEARANCE OF A GARMENT. AT FIRST GLANCE, THIS LOOKS LIKE AN IVORY BLOUSE UNDERNEATH A HIGH-BUTTONED TAN VEST. COLOR BLOCKING WITH HIGH OR LOW CONTRAST COLORS, PRINTS OR SOLIDS OFFERS SO MANY POSSIBILITIES FOR DIFFERENT EFFECTS. IN ADDITION, IT'S A PERFECT SOLUTION TO THE CHALLENGE OF CREATING A STYLISH GARMENT WHEN YOU DON'T HAVE ENOUGH YARDAGE FOR A PARTICULAR PATTERN.

Two "Soul Vests" from Lisa Mandle's Only One designer collection are both made out of linen, but are refreshingly different in the construction of their collars. Varying the details of a basic style—cuffs, collar, placket, yoke, pockets—offers tremendous creative possibility, and saves the time of experimenting with new and unfamiliar patterns.

BEGIN THE SEARCH FOR IDEAS IN YOUR CLOSET

You can start in your own closet, by evaluating the characteristics of the blouses you already own and love to wear the most. If you prefer a specific neckline style or type of fabric, use it as a starting point for inventive new directions. Or simply think about how a favorite blouse would look in a different fabric type or embellished with a great embroidery technique. The fashions on page 21 demonstrate how the very same blouse pattern can yield distinctively different results when some thought is given to creative variations.

Even your ready-to-wear shirts and blouses can stimulate new ideas. An interesting design detail on a store-bought blouse, such as contrasting bias bands or inventive color blocking, can be adapted to one of your own originals. Or use a purchased shirt as a clean slate for your creative talents and add a design detail or embellishment to make it as individual as you are. For example, a classic oxford button-down shirt takes on an artful and different effect if you add some interesting

schedule. You will quickly find that sparking your reserves of creative fuel ends up being a big time-saver, because you'll spend fewer hours searching the pattern books for a style that comes closest to what you've got in mind. Instead, you can apply your good ideas to patterns you already have—saving time and money! Just teach yourself to look at the whole world around you as your private laboratory for inventing new versions of old standby styles.

A Stitch in Time

Home decorating magazines or programs can be great sources for sewing ideas. Interesting color combinations, wallpaper patterns, upholstery trims, and window drapes can all be adapted to garments for dynamic effect.

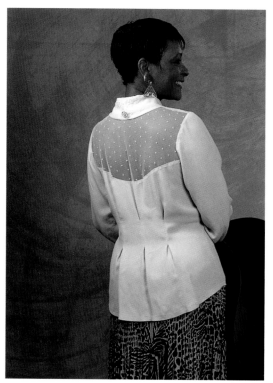

THESE TWO "FATE BLOUSES" FROM LISA MANDLE'S ONLY ONE COLLECTION MAY LOOK VERY DIFFERENT, BUT ARE ACTUALLY THE SAME DESIGN. THE OLIVE AND BURGUNDY VARIATION AT RIGHT IS CUT LONGER AND STRAIGHTER, HAS PATCH POCKETS, CONTRAST COLLAR, AND ELABORATE APPLIQUÉ TRIM AT THE BACK. THE IVORY MODEL IS PLEATED AT THE WAIST FOR A FORM-FITTING SILHOUETTE, HAS INTERESTING SHAPED POCKETS, AND A YOKE CUT FROM GOSSAMER TULLE.

embroidery motifs to the collar and cuffs, beadwork designs to the front button placket, or an abstract appliqué motif to the yoke. Start with a pared down classic and transform it into your own creation. You may have bought the core garment at the store, but you don't have to accept it as it is—top it off with your own design monogram!

While blouses beget other blouse ideas, don't ignore the dresses in your wardrobe during your tour. They can be inspiration for abbreviated blouse styles that you can quickly and easily adapt from the dress pattern. On the other hand, a favorite dress may cry out for a smashing overblouse or shirt-type jacket to perfect the total look. If you hadn't looked at the dress with a fresh eye and thought about how you might pair it with something unusual, you might not have otherwise been motivated to make the overblouse.

While you're still near your wardrobe, take a look at your sleepwear. A pretty nightgown, sleep shirt, camisole, or slip can inspire a blouse you'd wear outside the bedroom. Sleepwear can be a useful source of ideas for dreamy soft fabrics, feminine applications of trim, delicate stitching, and quick-to-assemble styles (after all, nighttime garments are rarely complicated in their construction). This type of blouse can be the perfect complement to a dressy jacket or sweater, for a very classy evening look.

CONSIDER THE ALTERNATIVES

A well-known phrase in the business and financial world is "What if?" We're advised to ask this question often, as a way to stimulate our consideration of all alternatives. This question is very useful during your tour of the world's creative laboratory. While you're still near the closet, start considering different aspects of favorite garments and ask the question, "What if?" What if you shaped the back yoke of that favorite western shirt and echoed the shape with similar embroidered motifs on the front pockets? What if you lengthened the front panels of that oxford shirt style to form a casual tie-front version? What if you

A Stitch in Time

People watch for pleasure and creative stimulation. When you see a great design or wardrobe idea, jot it down and refashion it later into one of your own originals.

combined the tuxedo front tucks of one blouse with the pleated collar of another? What if you attached long sleeves to a simple jewel-neck shell with pretty buttons at the shoulder, instead of setting them in the armhole permanently?

If you keep asking the question and stretching the borders of what's possible or conventional, you will quickly arrive at some very unusual combinations and variations. It's a type of brainstorming session with yourself and your clothes, allowing every possibility to be considered, despite its silly or outrageous first impression. Pile up the ideas as you arrange your clothes on the bed in different combinations. You will come to view your own closet as a storehouse of creative potential.

VISIT THE SEWING ROOM

Before you head out into the world on your search for creative stimulation, make a stop in your sewing area. Pull out your tried-and-true patterns and refresh your memory about why you like them so much. Then ask the leading question: What if? What if you made that blouse with a mandarin collar instead of a Peter Pan collar? Or perhaps that perfectly-fitting camp shirt pattern could be lengthened and cut larger to make a jacket. Or consider variations such as extending a blouse's right front and lapping it over the left, substituting different sleeve styles, or making a detachable overlay in a sheer fabric. You might even abbreviate a favorite shirt pat-

GIBSON GIRL
Blouse

STUDENTS IN A DYEING CLASS AT THE FIBER ARTS INSTITUTE IN DUNEDIN, FLORIDA TURNED THEIR CUSTOM FABRIC DESIGNS INTO VERY DIFFERENT BLOUSES. LEFT TO RIGHT: MARYELLEN TULLY DRESSED UP A SIMPLE T-SHIRT STYLE WITH A PAINTED PASSION FLOWER DESIGN. THERESA DAVIS TOPPED OFF HER SIMPLE "FITS ALL" TUNIC DESIGN WITH ELEGANT FROG CLOSURES. THELMA MATTHEWS FASHIONED HER SHIBORI-DYED CRINKLE FABRIC INTO A SHORT JACKET THAT LOOKS SHIRRED, BECAUSE THE CRINKLES CREATED BY THE DYEING TECHNIQUE WERE HELD IN PLACE WITH A LIGHTWEIGHT FUSIBLE INTERFACING. SHERRY FENNESSY CONTRASTED HER DYED IRIS AGAINST A RICH AND WARM YELLOW, AS INTENSE IN COLOR AS AN IRIS PETAL. DONNA McMANAMON ADDED LACE CAP SLEEVES AND A LACE INSERT AT THE FRONT HEM OF HER PULLOVER BLOUSE.

This famous turn-of-the-century blouse style was characterized by a high, closely fitted neck, finely embroidered or trimmed bodice, and long sleeves. The ideal Gibson Girl look was completed with long, flowing skirts and big, plumed hats or hair piled on the head in a bun. The style was named after American illustrator Charles Dana Gibson, who created the character in pen and ink drawings for various contemporary magazines from the 1890s into the early 1900s. Gibson Girls were often portrayed as modern aristocrats—poised, independent women who rode bicycles and traveled about unescorted. This image was quickly adopted by manufacturers of clothing and household to advertise their wares.

A Stitch in Time

When thinking up new ideas, consider all
the alternatives. Ask the question "What if?"
Consider every possibility and the best
ideas will emerge.

tern, by omitting the collar or turning it into a dickey that you wear under another garment.

And, finally, cast a loving glance at your stashed fabrics to see if any of them inspire a novel blouse treatment. A sleek silk might finally suggest making it up into an uncluttered sheath top that you can accent with braid or ribbon trim that swirls around the hem. Several related prints might cry out to be pieced together in a country-western shirt. Or, you might suddenly visualize some long-stored lace as the sleeves on a solid chiffon blouse. Consider all the possibilities. You will find that some of the ideas fade away and others keep coming back.

PEEK IN THE LINEN CLOSET

Browsing in thrift shops and antique stores for vintage napkins, placemats, and tablecloths that can be incorporated into wearables is all the rage today. The home style magazines regularly feature articles about collecting antique linens or decorating with interesting household textiles. Your own treasure trove of stained or slightly damaged linens can be explored for garment possibilities. The embroidered corners of

A Stitch in Time

Thrift store treasures and yard sale finds
can be beautifully recycled for fabric
pieces, buttons, and unusual trims. Vintage
linens, laces, and household textiles can
enjoy new life as garment collars, yokes,
plackets, and insertions.

an old napkin can enjoy a new life as the collar points of a linen blouse and an especially attractive heirloom tablecloth can be resurrected as a shirt. You might appreciate your family linens more in their new wearable versions than folded up and gathering dust in the linen closet or awaiting mending in your sewing room.

SCAN THE MAIL

Although mail solicitations and catalogs often take more time and space than they deserve, such materials can be sources of design ideas. Before you toss out any unwanted catalog, flip through the pages and keep your eyes open for interesting color combinations, design details, clothing ideas, or new accessories. Even if you have no use for a sweepstakes vacation invitation or a flower catalog, you might see something you can adapt to fabric. However, if you have enough creative inspiration to last a lifetime, don't spend your precious time looking at this material when you can be sewing instead!

HEAD OUT THE DOOR

To continue your tour of the world of ideas, simply turn on your antenna during your daily activities. This requires no extra, time-consuming trips that compete with your already-busy schedule. Just remember that the world is a laboratory of ideas that you can draw on at any time, if you are receptive to everything you observe.

While you are running errands, dip into the fashion stores to see which styles are the current rage. Remember, the famous fashion designers are faced with the same challenge as you—redesigning classic styles with a fresh, new look. Unusual combinations of color and texture, offbeat designs in braid and trim, and changing silhouettes created by different

fabric choices are hallmarks of the big names. They, too, have to keep coming up with good ideas, so you might as well study their seasonal interpretations for details that will spark your own imagination. Don't pass up the ethnic clothing or bridal stores, as they can be gold mines of ideas for unusual treatments and unpredictable contrasts.

When you visit your local sewing center, make note of the garment models the staff has on display. These are often the latest and newest styles from the various pattern companies, and some of their features might look particularly appealing to you. Check the new pattern books for new styles, new variations of old themes, and ideas you can develop from the patterns you have at home.

If you frequent antique stores, yard sales, or thrift shops, look for vintage fabrics or garments that can be recycled. A beautiful collar from an otherwise useless dress can be attached to a new blouse body. A gorgeous but out-of-style skirt might

MARY RUSSELL DOUBLED THE CREATIVE EXPRESSION OF THIS WESTERN SHIRT, BY MAKING TWO DIFFERENT BIBS. FOR A CHANGE OF PACE, SHE SIMPLY TAKES ONE BIB OFF AND BUTTONS ON THE OTHER ONE. SHIRT STYLES WITH FRONT BIBS OR PANELS ALSO PROVIDE A NICE SHOWCASE FOR EMBROIDERY OR APPLIQUÉ TALENTS.

A Stitch in Time

Look for good ideas in your own closet. Figure out why some garments are your favorites, and use those well-loved features again.

have enough fabric that it can be recut for a blouse. A damaged antique nightshirt can be trimmed down to make a camisole. Recycled household linens can be revived in all kinds of garments. Perhaps all you'll find are unattractive styles or damaged goods, but with great buttons. Don't pass them by. Instead, just cut off the buttons and add them to your collection; the price tag of the thrift shop item may well be far less than the cost of interesting new buttons. In the finer antique emporiums, you can study historic fashions and theatrical costumes for frills and stylings you might duplicate with modern materials.

When you're shopping for furniture or other household items, be alert to current colors and interesting upholstery details. Braid and piping trim on a couch can inspire innovative wearable

ELIZABETH SEARLE HAS MADE THE BLOUSE AT LEFT MANY TIMES, BECAUSE THE PRINCESS SEAMS ARE FLATTERING AND EASY TO ALTER FOR GOOD FIT. THIS TIME, SHE INSERTED SOME LACY GODETS IN THE SEAMS. THE RESULT IS A DRESSED-UP FEMININE LOOK WITH A PRETTY FLARED HEMLINE. A SOLID FABRIC FOR THE BLOUSE, CONTRASTED WITH A PRINT FOR THE GODETS, WOULD LOOK VERY DIFFERENT, AS IN THE BLOUSE ABOVE. SUCH SIMPLE ADDITIONS AND VARIED FABRIC COMBINATIONS CAN MAXIMIZE YOUR SEWING TIME BY GETTING THE MOST DESIGN POTENTIAL OUT OF A SINGLE PATTERN.

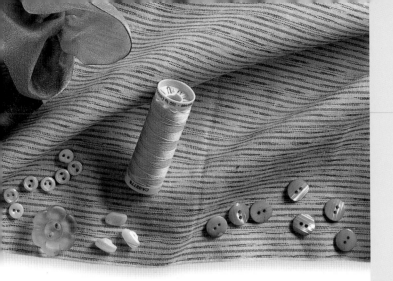

These two very different blouses were made from exactly the same pattern, proving that very different looks can be achieved without sewing entirely new pattern styles. Above, a creative combination of related fabrics accented with a stunning touch of red results in an Oriental graphic impression. Below, a romantic and feminine look is achieved with pretty pink fabric and floral appliqués. Most observers would not guess these are the same blouse styles.

These pretty blouses by Jean Davidson are made out of tucked fabric rectangles. The tucks provide shaping at the waist and shoulder and textural interest at the front opening and sleeve hem. The version on the left is made from hand-painted muslin, the one on the right is handkerchief linen. Worn buttoned up and by themselves, or unbuttoned and layered over other garments, these simple garments are truly versatile.

SHEILA BENNITT LOVES TO SEW AND PAINT. HERE, SHE COMBINES HER TWO CREATIVE PASSIONS IN AN OUT-OF-THE-ORDINARY, DRAMATIC OUTFIT. THE SERGED SEAMS ON THE OUTSIDE, STITCHED IN VARIEGATED THREAD, UNDULATE AMONG THE PAINTED STROKES AND PRINTED SHAPES.

useful sources of ideas you can apply to your sewing, particularly when it comes to arrangements of color and pattern. Check past volumes of books and periodicals that are filled with out-of-style ideas you can update for today, or simply wait a few years until they come back in fashion.

PEOPLE-WATCH FOR PLEASURE AND CREATIVE REJUVENATION

Natural curiosity makes people-watching a common activity, but it can be productive, too. Every day you will probably see evidence that the creativity in people is abundant and diverse, especially in the way they express themselves with their clothing and how they put outfits together. When you see something pass by that makes you stop and think, "What a great idea!," file the idea away or jot it down so you can remodel it later into something of your own. If your community or local shopping mall offers periodic fashion shows, try to attend and see what's coming down the runway. Otherwise, check in with the weekly style shows on television to keep up with how the designers are coping with the challenge of being creative. They draw on the world around them for inspiration and creative rejuvenation every season, so you should, too.

REFRESH YOUR SEWING TECHNIQUE

A half-day seminar or weekend class can do more to reenergize your sewing creativity than just about anything. If your schedule allows, try to take the time to learn at least one new technique every year. The surge of fresh possibilities that can

seam treatments, and draped window treatments can suggest manipulated fabric techniques. File these observations away in your mind's idea bank, for later reference, or in a small notebook you carry everywhere.

The home decorating and gift stores can also be searched for ready-made items that you will use only for their fabric. High fashion scarves, table dressings, and discontinued designer bed linens all provide enough material to cut some type of garment or garment section. While not always a less expensive alternative, such textiles often come in prints and textures not found in the fabric stores.

Spend a few extra minutes at the library, when you're picking up the latest novel or checking the stock market reports, and review the most recent fashion magazines for current approaches to color, fabric combinations, embellishment, and accessories. Even the home decorating magazines can be

A Stitch in Time

Refresh your sewing enthusiasm by
signing up for a class or checking out a
new book or video. Learning something
new is a great way to kindle
exciting new ideas.

come out of a class, even a very short one, will fire up an entire series of new projects. A two-hour seminar on pleating or a half-day sit-and-sew on machine embroidery will refresh your idea bank and you will then seek out opportunities to put your newly-learned skills to beautiful wear. Or sign up for that fitting class you've promised yourself for years, and the results will show in every new garment you make from that point on. If you're the type that learns well on your own, check out a new book or video and get ready to be excited and energized by the new ideas that will pour forth.

BUILD AN INSPIRATION LIBRARY

Keep track of all the good ideas you observe on your world tour by building your own inspiration library. Take notes of nifty ideas you see on people passing by or in library books, clip ads and photos from magazines or mail, and pin up swatches of fabric that you've got stashed. Assemble a scrapbook or organize file folders in your sewing area that you can go through when you need a boost, or hang a bulletin board so you can pin up a changing array of stimulating images—like those on pages 10 and 24. The more you surround yourself with the raw material of creative expression, the more fruitful your own ideas will become. And you'll find that, years later, even when the trends or fashions in your private idea library go out of style, you'll still be able to see in them a timeless detail or eye-catching ornament that will be useful in your own contemporary creations.

Creativity and the ability to think up new ideas isn't acquired by completing a course of study or getting certification. The skills of imagination and ingenuity aren't hereditary. Instead, restocking your private idea library with visionary, inventive possibilities will happen automatically when you turn on all your receptors and observe promising expressions of creativity in the world around you. This makes daily living a truly profitable adventure—one that will pay off when you get back to your sewing machine.

A Stitch in Time

Save the time of sewing the blouse and
purchase a plain style. Then, turn it into a
designer original with your own beautiful
beaded, appliquéd, or embroidered
inspirations.

GET SET...

For Efficient Sewing

Once you're fired up with plenty of good ideas, inspired by images like these, the challenge you face is finding the time and space to sew. If you are like most women, you're probably already over-committed and life is filled with plenty of activities, responsibilities, and an over-booked schedule. And, like most already-busy women, you probably manage to complete just about everything on your list—except finding more time to sew.

However, just as you refueled your creative resources while going about your daily business, you can organize your sewing to dovetail perfectly with your lifestyle. The key is to get organized, and, again, this doesn't require self-study courses or a certification seminar. You can simply assess your

daily workload, identify the fragments of uncommitted time (tiny as they may be), and reserve them for yourself and your sewing. It simply takes the motivation (never a problem for sewers!), determination, and a bit of strength to resist the pressures of the office, classroom, house, or garden during your reserved stitching time.

Once you have flagged the minutes or hours available for sewing, you can get even more mileage out of your stitching time by employing different efficiency tips during the stages of pattern and fabric selection, preparation for sewing, and the entire construction and finishing process. You will likely never find a way to devote entire days or weekends to sewing, so you might as well dismiss that as a dream and get on with a realistic approach. The best solution is to make the most of the time you do have—you will be surprised at how much sewing you can actually get done in the long run.

BLOUSE STYLES FOR MAXIMUM EFFICIENCY

When time is limited, don't use it up unraveling the mysteries of untried or complicated patterns. Instead, choose your favorite pared down, simple styles and then draw on your idea bank for creative touches that add the drama, glamour, or detail. Blouses may seem like abbreviated versions of dresses, and therefore should go together in a snap. But they can take a lot of time if the style is heavily tailored or has many complex seams. Therefore, if you need to finish a blouse this weekend, it's better to look for uncluttered and easy-to-assemble designs. Review your inventory of patterns for old standbys that fit well, go together easily, and look great. Use these as your starting points and then consider how you can vary them for novel results. For example, you might experiment with interesting fabric treatments, minor alterations to collars or hemline shape, or combinations with garment parts from other patterns.

Follow your instincts gained from hard experience when evaluating patterns for quick and problem-free assembly. Look over the pattern instructions, keeping an eye out for the assembly steps that are your most and least favorite. If you hate putting together tailored collars and lapels, select styles with simple necklines. You can dress them up later with scarves, overlays, and accessories, so don't spend precious time working on something you don't enjoy. For maximum productivity, avoid complicated seam treatments, styles with numerous pattern pieces, and lengthy finishing steps—and consider how you can use your sewing machine or serger features to further streamline construction.

Finally, stick with the styles you know will be flattering—you will enjoy sewing them and love wearing them. Plus, you won't run the risk of spending time on a garment only to have it hang in the closet. If you are like most sewers, you have already wasted time and fabric making up a pattern you knew in your heart was not the best choice for your figure. However, you may tell yourself that it's in style this season, the delectable fabric will "make" the garment, or you will lose five pounds before you finish it. All the rationalization in the world will not make a flattering garment out of a style that just doesn't work on you. See pages 26-28 for some reminder tips about flattering blouse styles.

If necessary, revisit your closet and try on your favorite clothes. Study yourself in the mirror and remind yourself exactly why you love them. Is it because of the fabric you chose, the flattering silhouette, the neckline shape, hemline length, color scheme, or the fact that it goes perfectly with a scarf or necklace in your collection? Armed with this knowledge, return to your pattern review and pull out the ones you know will produce new wardrobe favorites.

MIX, MATCH, AND LAYER

The beauty of sewing blouses is that they will be worn with companion garments, such as skirts, jumpers, slacks, vests, and jackets. Therefore, their designs do not always have to quite "stand on their own" as complete expressions of fashion flair. Remember this when you're selecting patterns for your next blouse projects. Consider how a particular blouse or shirt will be worn and think ahead about which pattern styles will be easy and quick to make, and will mix best with companion pieces already in your closet or on your "To Sew Next" list.

If you intend to always wear a selected blouse under a jacket or sweater, then choose a pattern with a simple straight sleeve or substitute sleeve styles to get the easiest variety. Or sew up just a few blouses with the simplest neckline styles as foundation garments for your whole collection of scarves, vests, shawls, and art-to-wear jewelry. You can even dispense with the majority of the blouse and cut the pattern down to a dickey, as on pages 56 and 68. If you want to create a number of looks with a blouse, consider making just one basic "core garment" and then assemble a wardrobe of detachable collars to vary the final appearance. Or turn a favorite shirt pattern into the perfect overblouse for your new slacks simply by cutting it longer and a bit wider. These are

A Stitch in Time

Enhance your efficiency by staying away from complicated garments and lengthy finishing steps. Start with a basic easy-to-assemble pattern and create interest with a simple, yet dramatic touch.

STYLES THAT FLATTER YOU

fast and efficient ways to guarantee that your tried-and-true, dependable patterns will always interface with the rest of your wardrobe—with versatility and grace.

A shirt or blouse covers only part of your figure, and it attracts particular attention to your face and upper body. Its style can, therefore, enhance or detract from your overall appearance. Even for this partial garment, it's worth remembering the various tips and rules about figure flattery you've probably heard

before. You will save time, and plenty of agony, if you stick with the styles that look best and do the most to attract attention to your best characteristics. The biggest time waster of all is making clothes that you never wear, because they don't look right or fit properly. Such garments sabotage your best efforts to create an attractive wardrobe. An endless stream of them will eventually squelch your creative sewing spirit. Keep in mind the following general rules for a flattering impression when choosing patterns and styles for your blouse and shirt fashions.

Vertical lines draw the eye upward and provide the illusion of greater height

Verticals can be obvious, as in striped fabric or fabric panels in different colors, or more subtle, such as topstitched or princess style seams and front plackets. Vertical elements can be accentuated with topstitching, piping, pleats, and buttons. If you want to appear taller and detract from wide figure features, such as wide hips or shoulders, think up-and-down.

Horizontal lines draw the eye sideways and provide the illusion of greater width

Such lines can be created by stripes, crosswise ruffles, and a prominent division at the hipline. If you are tall, but without much waist or hip definition, use horizontal features to give the illusion of a curvier figure. Otherwise, stay away from horizontal stripes (especially at the hips) and outfits that change color at the widest points of your figure.

Diagonal and asymmetrical lines can effectively divert the observing eye away from less than desirable characteristics

Additionally, because they can be surprising and unexpected, diagonals and asymmetrical styles enhance an overall effect, rather than specific areas. For example, a wide boat-neck shirt will draw attention to the shoulders while an asymmetrical neckline shape will attract attention to the entire upper body, because the observing eye will move back and forth along the lines rather than settling at the shoulders. Both diagonals and asymmetrics can add definition if the lines are sharply angled, contrasted against other garment features, or executed in crisp fabric; on the other hand, they lend a softer, more fluid look in drapey fabrics, monochromes, and gentle curving lines. Bias-cut styles are essentially diagonals, because the fabric is clearly neither vertical nor horizontal, which is how they create a fluid, pliable impression.

Exaggerated details add volume and weight, while stripped-down, spare styles reduce

Roomy cargo pockets at the hipline of a pair of slacks will add width, whereas in-seam pockets or none at all will create a sleek, slimming effect. Lots of ruffles, flutters, gathers, and puffs around the neckline will enhance a small bosom, but magnify a large one.

Dark colors and solids generally are slimming, while lights, brights, and prints add weight

If you coordinate a dark-colored outfit with matching slacks or hose, you will appear both thinner and taller; this is because the observing eye sees a long column of unbroken color. If you fear that darks, especially blacks, will make you appear too pale, soften their effect with texture (velvets, tweeds, rib knits) or style lines (bias-cut, curved, asymmetrical). You can also create softening transitions with a patterned silk scarf at the neck, a wrapped suede sash at the waist, a subtly contrasting overgarment, or unobtrusive jewelry. If you choose lights or pastels, make sure they contrast enough with your skin tone so that you don't "disappear" into the garment color. An ivory or tan that exactly matches your skin tone, or a white that's nearly identical to your teeth, robs you of interesting contrast.

Necklines make a frame for the face

A blouse or shirt is usually the garment that's worn closest to your face, so its style can be a useful tool for playing up your ideal characteristics and downplaying the traits you'd prefer to do without. A high, close-in neckline will immediately draw the observing eye to your face, whereas a boat neckline will accentuate your shoulders and a scoop neck will draw the eye to your neck and upper chest area. A V-neck will flatteringly accentuate a statuesque neck and will make a short neck appear longer. Stand-up and other tall collars tend to make a short neck disappear, creating the effect that the ears and shoulders touch each other; a classic collar or simple V-neck is preferable.

Shoulders support the entire look

Some fashion designers report that they begin at the shoulders and let every other detail of the garment flow from that

A Stitch in Time

If your arms are long, don't wear three-quarter length sleeves. It will look like you mistakenly cut the sleeves too short. If your upper arms are on the heavy side, stay away from cap sleeves—they accentuate the weight.

point. Your shoulders, in concert with your posture, do more to create your figure's overall impression than anything else. All clothes hang from them and because they're adjacent to the face, shoulders are usually where observers' gazes alight. Luckily, pattern styles can be selected and easily altered to emphasize straight, broad shoulders, augment narrow shoulders, and even out sloping shoulders. The various neckline styles (boat, jewel, V-neck, scoop) all affect your appearance at the shoulder line and your personal sewing experience will lead you to choose the most flattering variations. Shoulder pads, available in many different shapes, sizes, and degrees of softness, are an important tool in your figure flattery strategy, because they contribute a sharply defined or softer contour depending on what your upper body needs to project your desired image.

Sleeve styles are also important at the shoulder and should be chosen on the basis of the desired result. For example, dolman and raglan sleeve styles are a bit risky for someone with sloping shoulders because they accentuate the downward direction from neck to arm; this figure characteristic benefits from the more defining, set-in sleeve along with shoulder pads to create a straighter line from the neck. On the other hand,

kimono or raglan styles look great on figures that have broad, straight shoulders; a bonus is that the diagonal sleeve direction leads the eye toward the face—a focal point of your presentation to the world.

A well-fitting bust area improves a garment's hang or drape

The bust area is one of the most challenging to fit properly, because the fashion industry "standard" or "average" is usually not like a real body. However, pattern styles can ingeniously maximize or minimize your natural curves and should be evaluated for your individual physique. For example, a princess seam garment is quite flattering to all women (perhaps this is why most wedding gowns are princess styles) and can be easily altered to fit unique measurements. Blouse styles with bust darts typically will hang better on a curvy torso, while no-dart garments work well for less contoured figures. Smaller busts can be enhanced with bodice details such as ruffles and bows, while large busts are served better by sleek and simple vertical lines. It's well worth constructing a custom fitting pattern or muslin, at least for the bodice, and altering it until it fits you perfectly. Then, you will know the modifications

you have to make to every fashion pattern—saving you fitting time later on and guaranteeing a beautiful, flattering fit.

A QUESTION OF BALANCE

A key to overall figure flattery is to achieve balance among the various individual characteristics of your physique. For example, if you are wide-hipped, you won't want to echo that horizontal dimension with broad, padded shoulders. If you are short-waisted, you won't want to further condense your up-and-down dimensions with a belted-at-the-waist, bloused style; uninterrupted vertical lines and a belt below the waist are a better choice. If your upper arms are a bit heavy, don't ask everyone to notice them by wearing cap sleeves. If your arms are long, don't let them stick out of three-quarter length sleeves, because it will appear that you made a mistake and cut the sleeves too short. Use your own valuable sewing experience and attentive pattern selection to visually coordinate the various aspects of your figure into a well put together presence. Visit your local sewing shop or library for books that review the various principles of wardrobe planning for optimum personal style. Once you know what works best, stick with these predictable results and use your sewing time productively to repeat success over and over.

CARDIGAN
A British War Hero

Today, the cardigan is a collarless style with a straight, buttoned front opening. The original cardigan, however, had a collar. It was a knitted military jacket named after James Thomas Brudenell, the Seventh Earl of Cardigan (1797-1868). Earl Cardigan, a British officer and popular hero of the Crimean War (1853-1856), led the Charge of the Light Brigade and enjoyed brief fame for this military success. The woolen jacket he wore in the Crimea was copied soon after his return to London and sold by the thousands. The style has persisted through the centuries and was especially popularized by Chanel's famous wool cardigan jackets trimmed with braid. Incidentally, the Crimean village of Balaclava, site of the Charge of the Light Brigade, became the namesake for the knitted head covering worn by the soldiers. Today, the balaclava is commonly seen on skiers, cyclists, and other winter sports enthusiasts.

A Stitch in Time

If your space is as limited as your time, let the existing storage areas of your home do double duty. Store cutting and marking tools in the pantry, pressing supplies in the laundry room, and rolls of fabric in the bedroom (you'll dream about creating beautiful fashions).

CHANGING CONTOURS OVER TIME

As the years go by, you will undoubtedly notice inevitable changes in the measurements, contours, and general silhouette of your figure. These changes are pre-programmed into your genetic code and there just isn't much you can do to stop them from happening. You can learn, however, to adjust to your changing figure with poise and grace. To ensure that your patterns and garments continue to be the most flattering they can be, learn how to make some basic alterations to accommodate physical changes. Periodic updates of your body measurements and alteration of your fitting muslin, or sloper, if you use one, is a worthy investment of time and can save you many hours and considerable aggravation in the long run. Check out a book on custom fitting or enroll in a class at your local sewing center or community college to learn these easy skills that make all the difference in your life-long appearance. See page 47 for some fitting challenges that are common to blouses and shirts.

EVALUATING PATTERNS FOR CREATIVE ADAPTATION

Once you have narrowed down your pattern possibilities to those few that are quick and easy to assemble, and attractive to wear, think how you can maximize your sewing time by making them over and over again, but varied creatively for distinctively different results. The patterns you already own are a valuable resource for creative design, and using them more than once saves money and shopping time. An easy way to begin is to consider how to make the same pattern in different ways, so you can wear the resulting garments together or separately. For example, make your favorite T-shirt pattern as is; then, make it again in a roomier, longer version, but lower the neckline or change its shape and omit the sleeves. You now have a tunic you can wear over the T-shirt, with other garments, or by itself under a long jacket. The same pattern in two slight variations, sewn in assembly-line fashion, creates several new wardrobe possibilities for your closet. Similar options include shortening an easy dress pattern to make a blouse, enlarging a blouse pattern to make a jacket, and paring down a nightgown pattern to make a camisole.

Study the lines of your selected pattern for reshaping opportunities. An undulating shirt hem can be more interesting than one that is straight around the figure, and it doesn't cut across the body as dramatically. Seamlines can be accentuated with piping, trim, or mirror-image rows of beads. Sleeve hems can be shaped or varied with pulled thread or cutwork designs, or the sleeves can be cut along the selvage of a pretty, scalloped fabric for a beautiful no-finish edge. The Heirloom

Camp shirt on page 66 and the Eyelet Confection blouse on page 81 illustrate the attractive results of these easy variations. Look for ways to replace complicated, time-consuming features with quicker substitutes, such as bias bands instead of cuffs and neckline edgings instead of collars. These are just a few of the inventive methods of creating a custom original from an old faithful pattern that is also quick to assemble.

Notice the open expanses of your pattern styles and use them as a showcase for decorative stitching, unusual appliqué, and other special effects. A brief amount of time spent embellishing a collar, yoke, or front panel can yield a spectacular final effect. Or split a large piece into smaller components, and reassemble it with different colors, textures, or designs. The Marbled Icing blouse on page 79 and the Sedona Sunset tunic on page 108 illustrate this approach to creating interest with custom-pieced material.

Study your patterns for fabric manipulation possibilities, which take a simple style into bold new design territory. Pleating, smocking, and tucking texturize any garment surface in an unexpected way. Fabric painting, dyeing, and stamping let you design your own prints. Juxtaposing reversible fabrics results in subtle color plays, while arranging stripes, polka dots, and other symmetrical prints creates a bold and visually exciting assemblage. Inserting lace and trim between garment pieces, a common heirloom technique, can be updated for a very modern classic. Appliqué, embroidery, and other surface decoration all add a special texture to an otherwise plain piece of cloth.

As you can see, the simplest of patterns can become mini-laboratories for decorative experimentation. All of the designs in this book were created by sewers like you, who wondered how to add pizzazz to a basic style. They studied the patterns, considered all the alternatives for innovative interpreta-

A Stitch in Time

To evaluate the best neckline shapes for your figure, study your favorite blouses for their neckline features or drape a necklace or length of drapery weights in different arrangements until you identify the most attractive shape.

tion, and maximized their sewing time to just get it done. When you pair your own tried-and-true patterns with great ideas from your inspiration library, and put efficiency to work at the sewing machine, every garment you make will be a beautiful expression of your own creative style.

FINDING THE TIME TO SEW

When you're bursting with ideas and the creative energy is flowing, it's sometimes difficult to get a handle on things, know exactly where to start, and get down to the business of sewing. This is where organization can be your best sewing ally. By scheduling your time efficiently and ordering the sewing process effectively, you will need less time to turn the inspiring visions in your mind's eye into real garments you can wear next week. You will get more sewing done because you will make the most out of the limited time you have.

Time is the most precious commodity we've got, and the one we can never get enough of. It's every sewer's dream to have days of free time, entire weekends and vacations of commitment-free hours to spend cutting, sewing, embellishing, and dreaming about the next fabulous creation. However, dreams are usually far from reality, and you have to live with the fact that any sewing time you manage to get, you generally have to carve out of an overbooked daily or weekly schedule. The time commitments required by family, workplace, school, church, and home are tremendous, leaving precious little for personal interests, not to mention exercise, self-improvement, entertainment, and sleep.

While you may find this real-world scenario extremely depressing, it is a fact of life in the modern age. Labor- and time-saving gadgets that maximize our productivity also encourage us to achieve even more. Stores that stay open around the clock invite us to get chores done during hours we

A Stitch in Time

Schedule stitching activities in your calendar, right next to medical appointments or meetings. Sewing is just as important to your overall well-being and deserves its own allocations of time, even if it's only 30 minutes.

used to spend relaxing. Relaxation has somehow ended up with a bad name in today's active, achievement-oriented society, even though we all yearn for more time to do just that. Numerous options for entertaining ourselves, from television to the Internet, tempt us away from the sewing room where a difficult assembly step may be waiting. Sewing projects get derailed because of many good, and not so good, reasons: a parent-teacher conference at school, an evening class, an important deadline at work, a pressing family affair, or just a great movie on TV. Sewing tends to be delayed over and over, in favor of the "more important" commitments.

The key to getting organized for productive sewing is to convince yourself absolutely that sewing is one of those important

commitments that you always manage to find time for. Therefore, it deserves the same scheduling attention that other areas of your life receive. Whether it's your personal therapy, your fun time, creative outlet, or source of family clothing, the time you get in the sewing area is crucial to your well-being. All artists and crafters who are passionate about what they do understand this link to overall well-being. And there is no question that most sewers are passionate about what they do. Therefore, make this activity a priority in your daily life!

STAKE OUT TIME AND PUT IT ON THE CALENDAR

When you've convinced yourself that needle and thread time is extremely valuable, you're faced with a simple logistical challenge—how to get more hours with your hands on the fabric. First, don't wait for free time to present itself. Be an active explorer of your daily life, in search of minutes and segments of hours that could be put to use in other ways. If you spend too much time every evening shopping and preparing dinner, promise yourself a weekly menu planning session on Saturday morning; then do the requisite shopping and any convenient advance food prep before the weekend ends, leaving your weekday evenings just a little more open-ended than before. You can then apply that newly available time to make progress on your sewing projects, instead of let-

A Stitch in Time

Refuel your stores of creative energy with a bulletin board of images from your inspiration files. When you're doing monotonous work, a quick glance at the board will keep you thinking about exciting new ideas.

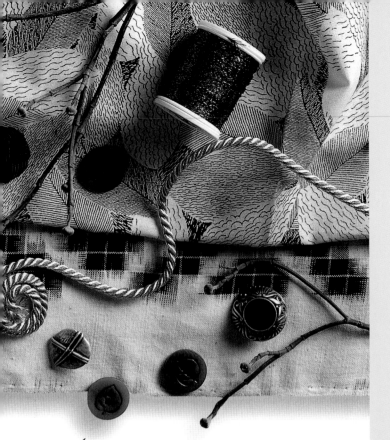

The Raglan Sleeve
Innovation in Battle Garb

A Stitch in Time

Sew for the real you—don't waste precious time on styles that don't flatter your figure. Use your fashion originals to make the most of your good features.

ting it dribble away on other distractions. Nearly every one of the blouses in this book is organized according to a weekly plan that schedules garment construction to match the available time during the week, and to be ready to wear by the end of the weekend.

Next, note all available time slots, no matter how brief, in whatever time-management or scheduling system you use for your professional career or other commitments of life. Write it down in a date book, circle the times on a calendar, or dictate a memo to yourself on your personal recorder. If a 45-minute dental cleaning deserves an entry in your scheduling system, then a 30-minute entry for picking up interfacing at the store, studying your next "To Sew" pattern, or spending

The raglan sleeve is cut in one with the shoulder area and joined to a garment by a diagonal seam that runs from the underarm to the neckline. This style provides a looser fit and greater mobility in the shoulder/arm area, which was the incentive for its development. It was named for Fitzroy James Henry Somerset, the First Baron Raglan (1788-1855), a British Commander during the Crimean War. He had the sleeves of his military uniforms altered after having an arm amputated at Waterloo; the altered jacket became known as a raglan coat. Raglan did not enjoy the popular fame of his military contemporary, the Earl of Cardigan, because the glory of Cardigan's Charge of the Light Brigade overshadowed the battles of Raglan's freezing, starving, and diseased troops. Raglan died in the Crimea in June, 1855.

time at the machine belongs there, too. If you're uncomfortable mixing personal activities with professional commitments, then redefine your sewing terminology for greater stature. Use reminder words such as "Design Time" for hours spent at your machine, "Style Consulting" for the lunch hours when you cruise through the mall looking for good ideas, or "Technical Study" for the seminar or sit-and-sew you've enrolled in. If someone glances through your date book, you'll never feel the need to explain or defend the way you spend your time. You shouldn't have to rationalize your basic need to sew, but we all do it!

MATCH THE TIME TO THE JOB

Learn to flex with your available schedule and put every fragment of time to work, in the interest of completing your next garment or teaching yourself a new stitch technique. If Tuesday evenings yield only 15 free minutes in between previous commitments or family activities, select one operation from the vast inventory of sewing steps to complete in that time. See page 36 for a reminder about just how productive you can be in 15 minutes. Basting on a cuff or fusing two pieces of interfacing in place puts you closer to a finished garment, even if it is just a little bit. And bit by little bit, you will reach the final steps of construction—hemming, pressing, and wearing! If, on the other hand, you let too many of those brief segments get by, unfinished projects will languish in your studio and you will feel that you cannot get any sewing done.

When multiple hours or half-days unexpectedly open up, resist the urge to finish chores or give in to the tendency to say "I should do something productive, instead." If life will go on without getting those chores done, you'll be happier spending the time on major sewing production steps—cutting out a cou-

A Stitch in Time

Despite your diet and exercise regimen, your genetic code will cause gradual changes in your figure over time. Adjust to them with poise, grace, and a periodically updated master pattern or sloper.

ple of new patterns, pleating fabric for a shirt front, assembling a garment, redrafting a pattern, or other activities that require more significant amounts of attention. Then, when life gets back to normal and free time again comes only in short spurts, such as while dinner is cooking or you're waiting for the doctor, you can once more utilize the brief moments profitably on the small steps that remain after the big ones are completed.

DO DOUBLE DUTY

With an open mind and a little preparation, you can put time to work for you in more than one way. When you're shopping or traveling, keep an eye out for good ideas or scan the new season fashions for creative possibilities and jot them down in a notebook you keep handy at all times. When you're running errands, stop in at the fabric store to pick up the buttons you need; save the browsing for another, lengthier trip. If you know you'll be waiting while your car is serviced, plan ahead to carry along some small hand sewing. While the casserole is baking, slip into the sewing room to do a bit of stitching, or bring the pattern guide sheets into the kitchen and study them for more efficient construction or creative alteration.

SET UP YOUR SPACE FOR USER-FRIENDLY OPERATION

A common sewer's fantasy is to have unlimited time, but you've now given up that fantasy and you're back down to earth, organizing small chunks of time for optimum efficiency. However, you may be falling prey to another recurring dream: that of having unlimited space in which to sew. Again, the real-world conditions under which you get your sewing done are probably very different than your dreams of light-filled, roomy studio space that you don't have to share

A Stitch in Time

Don't let the briefs stints of time get by. If you've got only 15 minutes available to sew, put the time to good use by choosing a simple do-able task that advances your project toward completion.

A Stitch in Time

Study a basic pattern for creative variation like a shaped hem that undulates around the body or interesting seam treatments, such as piping or decorative topstitching.

with anyone. It's likely that you either have a tiny sewing room or that you must share space in another area of the house, such as the den or dining room. Either way, count yourself lucky if you have enough room to set up a machine—everything else can be improvised with a little organizational effort.

Just as the secret to productive sewing is to use the available time you manage to carve out of your busy schedule, efficient sewing depends on your ability to use any and all available space. It's not necessary to stake out an entire room, where every sewing activity can take place, because that isn't always possible in small houses or apartments. Instead, break up the overall sewing activity into smaller, more discrete tasks that can be dispersed over several areas. Then stroll around the house, basement, or garage and try to visualize where those tasks can be easily and efficiently accomplished. For example, the island in your kitchen can double as a cutting and marking area, the linen closet can store a box of patterns, the laundry alcove can house the ironing board and pressing supplies, and the bedroom can host a basket of rolled fabric (this may help you dream of beautiful new fashions while you sleep).

Then, you can organize the sewing supplies you need for each task to be nearby. If you cut out fabric at the kitchen counter, store your cutting and marking tools in a kitchen drawer or in the pantry. The measuring cups and cans of soup can be easily compressed into less shelf space to make room. Even though you'd rather have all sewing-related supplies and equipment in one dedicated place, there's no reason why you can't put your home's built-in kitchen, bath, and other storage space on double duty. If you worry that other cooks in the family will damage your kitchen-stored tools, protect them inside cannisters, plastic storage bags, cloth silverware bags, or clearly marked boxes.

The goal is to keep all supplies conveniently located when you need them, so you don't waste time gathering them from far-flung nooks and crannies of the house. If you're uncomfortable about dividing up your sewing equipment and spreading it around the house, then put together a toolbox that can be stowed out of harm's way. A large fishing tackle box, computer carrying case, or small suitcase on wheels will keep your treasured accessories handy, organized, and away from non-sewers. Then, when you're ready to cut, mark, and begin stitching, just set it up nearby. In tandem with a basket or box that holds your pattern, fabric, and notions, such a supply solution becomes a mobile sewing workshop.

If you're one of the lucky ones to have a room all to yourself, try to arrange it for the greatest measure of efficiency. Think about the natural flow of your sewing and set up equipment to go along with it—serger next to standard machine, ironing board nearby, bobbins and threads within reach—so you won't waste minutes or motion as you proceed from step to step. This is what time-motion experts do when they are asked to consult with factory executives, in order to increase worker productivity or streamline assembly procedures. You can do the same thing by evaluating your own energy output and

A Stitch in Time

Save the cost of specialty buttons by using a concealed placket. Sew on a single gorgeous button at the top, and hide inexpensive plain buttons within the placket.

then rearranging or setting up your sewing area to help you get more sewing done in less time.

Don't forget to build in a system for refueling your stores of creative energy. A bulletin board posted in full view and covered with inspiring sketches, swatches, or magazine clips will keep you thinking ahead. When you're doing monotonous work or executing a familiar step you could complete with your eyes closed, a glance at the board will occupy your mind, keep you focused on sewing, and stimulate new ideas. If you don't have room for a bulletin board, make a mini-showcase on the inside or outside of your mobile sewing kit.

KEEP YOUR INVENTORY WELL-STOCKED

When you're stitching away at top speed, you won't want to be rudely interrupted because of supply shortages. Running out of interfacing or not having the right lining can really dampen your spirits and interfere with your efficiency. The obvious preventative measure is to keep track of your notions and supplies, and stock up before you run out. Keep notes of needed accessories or collect swatches of used-up trims at the end of each sewing session, and carry them with you when you head out the next day. A lunch-hour jaunt to the sewing store or a quick stop between errands will fit easily into

15 THINGS YOU CAN DO *in 15 minutes*

1. Scan a fashion or home design magazine for good ideas to clip and file.

2. Study a favorite blouse pattern for creative alteration possibilities.

3. Organize your pattern and supplies for marking and cutting at your cutting area.

4. Press and straighten the grain of your fabric before cutting into it.

5. Redraw a new shaped sleeve and trace a pattern for it.

6. Sew a buttonhole, clip open, trim ends, and seal with fray retardant.

7. Stitch several samples of decorative motifs on different interfacings and stabilizers.

8. Stitch, trim, turn, and press a collar or cuff.

9. Start work on a pieced or faggoted fabric rectangle, to use for a blouse front or collar.

10. Stitch up a previously cut-out muslin sample bodice and try it on for fit.

11. Alter and redraw a pattern piece for a new neckline or concealed front placket.

12. Cut down a discarded blouse to make a dickey.

13. Start a soaking wash of vintage linens.

14. Update your blouse profile by taking new upper body measurements.

15. Try on favorite garments in your wardrobe to identify flattering styles.

your daily routine and guarantee that your basic supplies are at hand.

Of course, you don't have to turn off the lights just because you ran out of something. Seize the time and put it to good use. Look over your pattern construction steps and determine what else you can be doing, until you replace the missing or used-up items. Move on to the preliminary steps of your next project or force yourself to decide on which buttons to use on that recently finished jacket and sew them on. Or consider a sewing interruption as a blessing in disguise, and rejoin your loved ones or make a cup of tea to sip while you enjoy a few peaceful minutes for yourself.

A Stitch in Time

Stay up to date with sewing technology.
A new tool or sewing machine attachment
can save time, improve your technique, or
create a neat decorative effect.

KEEP UP WITH TECHNOLOGY

Speaking of supplies and equipment, be aware that manufacturers are constantly turning out new and improved gadgets to help you sew faster and better. It's worthwhile to keep up with what's available, because you may find some new marvel that will shave minutes off a least-favorite assembly step or a machine attachment that simplifies a complex operation.

A Stitch in Time

Stop dreaming about entire days and
weekends of free time for sewing. Instead,
learn to make the most of the time you do
have-you will be surprised at how much
you can get done.

Basting aids, tracing implements, rotary cutters, specialized sewing machine feet, and plenty of other notions are available at your local sewing center or through the mail order catalogs. You should periodically review what's new on the scene, so you won't miss out on something that can save you time, improve your skills, or make a process easier. The time you spend checking out new products or discussing industry advances with your sewing dealer will certainly benefit you in the long term and will be apparent in the technologically sophisticated styles you create.

Once you have your schedule under control, your sewing space deftly organized, and your supplies fully stocked, you're ready to forge ahead and start sewing. So get ready to see all your advance planning pay off, as you spend time doing what you love best—working with fabric to create beautiful expressions of who you are. Although you have laid the groundwork for efficient sewing, with your creative tour and expert planning, there is still plenty of opportunity to incorporate time-saving principles and touches of innovation during the preparation, assembly, and finishing stages.

A Stitch in Time

When choosing blouse patterns, think
about what you will wear the finished garment with. Don't bother with a complex collar if you're making the blouse to go with a
collection of scarves.

GET
READY
GET
SET
SEW!

The moment when you actually get to the sewing room is what you've worked so hard to attain. That moment is also very fragile, subject at any second to being claimed by some other concern, such as a family event, telephone call, or household emergency. And once you finally get to the machine or serger, the pressure to make the most of your time is tremendous, because you don't want to feel that you have wasted such precious minutes. But don't despair, the stitches will start to fly if you're well-prepared, your supplies are organized, and you are clear about the next step of the garment-assembly process. Armed with a pattern and inspiration, you're ready to begin creating fashions that will become your own wardrobe collectibles.

START OUT FIT AND TRIM

You will probably be sewing for your entire life, and you will probably always have limited time. When you consider your sewing career as a lifetime endeavor, the best long-term plan for efficient use of time is to concentrate on making styles that flatter you and then fitting them to your very individual figure. Don't avoid the fitting step by selecting patterns that are feature-less or loose and baggy. You will end up rejecting those garments once they are hanging in your closet because they just never seem to look right, feel right, or do anything to enhance your figure.

Even though you're anxious to begin stitching, the time spent in advance of sewing to achieve a perfect fit is a great investment in a fabulous overall look and a sure bet for saving time on each garment you then create. Clothes that fit you well make the most of your good figure characteristics, minimize your less-than-ideal traits, and are more comfortable to wear because they move with, not against, the natural contours of your body. It's no coincidence that well-fitting fashions also become your favorites.

Don't assume that the pattern companies manufacture a size that will fit you perfectly. It's impossible for any pattern-maker to standardize the world's individual shapes into one perfect-for-everybody silhouette. You're not standard and your individual measurements won't match the industry average, so face the fact that you may have to adjust every store-bought pattern in accordance with the real you. See page 47 for some common blouse-fitting challenges and solutions.

Bite the bullet and make a custom fitting pattern (also called a sloper) to fit your accurate measurements. If doing this on your own is anxiety-provoking, as it is for many sewers, sign up for a class or check out a fitting book. There are several old and new titles out there and you will certainly find one that is easy to follow and makes this subject approachable. It is not difficult, and once you've perfected that master fitting pattern, you will know how to adjust every single fashion garment you sew from then on, to conform to your unique physique.

If your measurements diverge greatly from a pattern's standard measurements, know that you will have to alter it, following your master pattern. If, however, your measurements don't differ too much, you can probably get by with the improvised alteration methods you've developed during your years of sewing. You might cut larger side seam allowances to allow for taking in or letting out later, make use of tucks and pleats to control volume, or graduate from one cutting line to another on a multi-size pattern.

You can also make a muslin sample of an individual pattern or your own original design, to pre-test it for fit and to judge its attractiveness on your figure. This is a quick and painless operation, usually requiring no more than an hour. Cut out enough of the pattern pieces to be able to assess the garment (you won't need the hem facings, cuffs, or some other non-essential pieces), mark construction features right on the muslin, and sew it together fast with long machine stitches (keep your seamlines accurate, however). You won't have to do any of the finishing work just to see how the garment will fit; trim off the hem allowance and don't bother with buttonholes. After a glance in the mirror, you will know whether you want to commit any more time, or fabric, to this style. If the answer is yes, you can proceed with confidence. If the answer is no, you can move on with relief, knowing you won't end up with another unwearable item.

Muslin is both inexpensive and widely available, which makes it ideal for sample-making. However, you could also start using up your bargain fabric stash for pretesting patterns or original garment designs. You will have to cut out all pieces and be a bit more careful with your marking and stitching, but if the sample passes the pretest you can go ahead and complete it. Instead of starting over with your fashion fabric, you'll have a ready-to-wear garment that began as a sample. Nobody but you will ever know.

Explore Creative Opportunities

The fitting or sample-making stage of your sewing is the perfect time to test opportunities for creative experimentation, as well as fit and appearance. If you're already making up a muslin, go ahead and reshape the sleeve or try out a new collar style to see if you like the results. You won't have to stop and do it later, possibly causing a glitch in the flow of your cutting and sewing. Just as it's always more efficient to have your fabrics and notions lined up in advance, it's better to have a good idea of how your pattern alterations and creative adaptations will work ahead of time. The designers of many of the blouses in this book recommend making advance samples, to test stitch technique, machine tension, pleating depth, dye effects, and many departures from the "as-is" pattern.

Fit Prep Steps into Your Daily Life

Fitting and sample-making are common preludes to all efficient sewing and so are the necessary preparation stages, such as pretreating fabric, reviewing your pattern's construction steps, and cutting and marking. Handle these various operations most efficiently by figuring out how to seamlessly coordinate them with your already-busy schedule. For example, during breakfast or while you're cooking dinner, start a small prewash load of fabric or preshrink interfacing and

A Stitch in Time

When sewing on four-hole buttons, use separate threads in the different pairs of holes. If one thread breaks or wears out, the other will hold it and you won't lose a button.

hang it up to dry. Straighten the grain of the fabric for your next project or press the wrinkles out in between loads of family laundry. Clean your sewing machine or wind a couple of bobbins while waiting for the car to warm up. These small, swift tasks can be completed during the briefest openings in your daily routine. Then, when you've got an evening hour or a Saturday afternoon, you will be well along the way toward completion.

Regardless of the specific strategy you use to dovetail these prep steps with your schedule, do not neglect them altogether, thinking you will save time later on. You won't, as you most likely have learned from your own experience. A garment made from off-grain fabric or material that was not pretreated can be a disaster. If not on grain, it won't hang right, no matter what you do. And the first laundering of a fabric that wasn't pretreated may cause shrinkage or colors that run. A sewing machine that is not regularly cleaned and oiled will eventually disappoint you, and will derail your sewing efficiency by damaging your fabric or breaking down completely. Don't risk a breakdown of your own by sacrificing the preparation steps because your time is limited. Instead, use every available minute to get ready for sewing, just as you did to stimulate your creativity and organize your equipment.

A Stitch in Time

Make different sizes of buttonhole samples on interfaced swatches of the fashion fabric before heading out to purchase buttons. You can button the samples right on top of the button cards or lay loose buttons on top, to identify the perfect match.

Study the blueprints for your garments ahead of time

The sample-making and preparation stages are excellent opportunities to familiarize yourself with the pattern and, particularly, to remind yourself about creative adaptations you will be making during construction. This built-in review process is a big time-saver, too. You won't have to stop and study the order of assembly steps, because making the muslin sample will still be fresh in your mind. Or, if you studied the pattern while your fabric was prewashing, you'll be familiar with the flow of assembly. It's helpful to mark right on the pattern guide sheets or make notes alongside about variations you'll be per-

A Stitch in Time

When space is limited, use all available nooks and crannies of your home to help with sewing supply storage. A mobile sewing kit in a toolbox or rolling suitcase makes fast work of collecting everything when you need it.

forming and where they fall in the order of construction, so you won't have to backtrack later because you forgot something.

You will notice that the construction of the garments in the Weekend Sewer's series is organized according to a "Plan for the Week." At a glance, you can tell what needs to be done each weekday evening, to ensure that the garment can be finished up over the weekend. If all that is scheduled for Wednesday evening is to pretreat your fabric, but you've got extra energy and time, then you can comfortably proceed to something else. But it's also nice to know that if you're low on energy and time, at least you can get the pretreating done and still complete the project by Sunday evening. Schedule each of your sewing projects this way and make entries on your calendar. You'll be surprised at how easy it is to stimulate sewing progress when you schedule it in do-able daily tasks, and you'll be delighted with the new fashions that flow out of your sewing room.

Reorder the construction process to suit you

The act of sewing is as individual as the styles you create and you should feel free to alter the process to fit your own preferences and work habits. The instruction sheets that come with commercial patterns describe the manufacturer's recommended procedure, but you don't have to be a slave to the recommendations. In fact, for the most efficient and time-saving stitching, the order of steps can be rearranged to match your own sewing style. For example, constructing and attaching a shirt collar are usually among the first steps of a pattern, while cuffs come much later. However, the similar stitch-trim-turn-press assembly technique of collars and cuffs can make it more logical to do both at the same time. Then, just set the cuffs aside until they are needed later. Or, stitch all the straight seams (back, side, underarm, for example) at the same time, and then press them in a group, instead of completing these tasks one by one, as outlined in most pattern instructions.

Comparable procedures that require similar types of attention and detail can be done together, to streamline the overall construction process. Again, the muslin sample-making stage is a perfect time to experiment with customizing the construction process to suit you. If the pattern you're using is a dependable, pretested model that doesn't require an advance

A Stitch in Time

Streamline your sewing by cutting out several projects in assembly line fashion. They will then be lined up and ready for you, whenever you can get to the machine.

sample, it's still wise to review the order of steps for possible adjustments to accommodate a particular embellishment technique or just to further speed construction along. Remember to make notes right on the guide sheets or a separate reminder slip, so you won't lose track of how you decided the pattern should go together.

This flexible approach to garment construction also makes it easier to integrate sewing into your unpredictable schedule. If you've got just a few minutes or you're tired and don't have the energy for assembling a complicated section, you can review the pattern and pick out the steps that match your available time and energy level. If you're next "To Do" step is the collar, but you're not in the mood for it, look ahead and pick out steps that are fun, quick, and stress-free, such as pockets or decorative embroidery details. Or, if you're ready for the hemming and buttonholes, but these are your least-favorite steps, set them aside until your next sewing session. Instead, get yourself excited and energized by organizing the fabric and notions for your next project. In the context of a lifetime of sewing, the order of completing these steps is not that significant. It won't matter that much if one blouse sits for weeks, awaiting the perfect buttons, while you move on to other garments. The goal is to use your limited time wisely, and to keep yourself inspired, excited, and sewing.

USE ASSEMBLY LINE PRINCIPLES

If you agree that the exact order of garment construction is flexible, then you can put the principles of assembly line productivity to work for you. Additionally, if you can keep track of three projects at once, then choose your patterns to coordinate with an assembly line approach. For example, apply three different ideas from your inspiration library to the identical shirt pattern. Cut them out at the same time and sew them

in assembly line fashion, completing each step one right after the other on the three models. You may have to make minor modifications to the order of construction, to incorporate the various decorative innovations, but that's no problem and the garments will go together faster than if you made them separately, because your assembly strategy is consistent and your stitching attention is focused on the one pattern style. The result? Three different looks made in less time than if you assembled each one separately from start to finish.

This streamlined approach is especially time-saving during the cutting and marking stages of sewing, particularly if you do not have a dedicated sewing room and you must set up your cutting/marking arrangement in another part of the house. It's more efficient to cut and mark several garments, while all supplies are right at hand, than one by one. When you move back to the sewing machine, you'll have several garments ready to go and you won't delay progress because of the inconvenience of clearing off the kitchen counter or getting out the cutting table.

And while you've got all your supplies spread out, don't forget to cut and mark linings, interfacings, cordings, and other components that will be difficult to do later in cramped quarters. This is the best time to pretest interfacings for fusing quality or compatibility with your fashion fabric; if your first choice doesn't look like it's going to work well, you can cut out a different type before you've put everything away. Besides, it's

nice to know that everything you will need for a project is prepared and ready for you.

SEARCH OUT RESOURCES FOR FASTER SEWING

Now that you are supremely organized, fired up with a great idea for some creative flair, armed with a pattern reordered for speedy construction, and confident that all prep steps are done, you are ready to apply the very same time- and labor-saving strategies to the actual stitching operation. If you learned how to sew from a relative or a home economics instructor, you undoubtedly and automatically internalized her favorite tips and tricks for faster sewing. It's wise, however, to realize that sewing technique develops and advances just like any other technology. Designers invent new and better ways to do things, inventive sewers develop accessories that save time or facilitate certain functions, and sewing machine manufacturers turn out new models that revolutionize stitching and construction.

While some effort is required (not to mention time) to change your routine and learn a new habit, you will profit in the long run if you can teach yourself some new hints for faster and better sewing. Study the "Stitch in Time" boxes and "Tips from the Designer" in this book or scan other volumes in your personal collection for helpful ideas. Visit your local sewing center or bookstore to review the new publications and videos; they often will reveal many new tricks for stitching efficiency. Or sign up for a sewing seminar, sit-and-sew class, or lecture by a visiting professional; these opportunities are fun and always invigorate you with creative ideas, tips, and information about new developments in the fashion world. You're bound to adapt some of what you learn to your own sewing

style and the result will inevitably be better-made garments sewn in less time.

Keep your eyes open for new supplies and equipment that can speed you up, make a complex operation easier to perform, or take the agony out of a dreaded construction step. You will find new tools for cutting, marking, basting, and stitching that are amazing in their ability to improve efficiency or quality. You can take advantage of new machine attachments that automate tedious hand sewing or complex embroidery. A periodic review of new developments in the tools of your trade will alert you to opportunities for better and more productive sewing.

While we're on the subject of tools, do remember that the most useful tools are those that are kept in good condition. Careful use and proper storage of your accessories guarantee that they will always be ready when you are and will enhance your productivity. Give your sewing machine and serger regular cleanings and dealer tune-ups so you can enjoy a lifetime of smooth and trouble-free stitching. Review your owner manuals to remind yourself about proper maintenance and also about the special effects you can achieve. Today's machines are so versatile and sophisticated that it's easy to forget all they can do.

A FABULOUS FINISH

Much like a cake that isn't quite finished until it's appropriately decorated, a garment isn't always finished when you've put in the last hem stitch or sewn on the final button. When you have reached the final stage of construction, you're faced with deciding on a final touch that distinguishes your original creation from the ranks of the ordinary. You may have planned the crowning touches of your garment in advance, such as interesting pattern alteration or fabric manipulation, and incorporated them into the construction process. If so, you're ready to show off your custom original to the world.

44

However, you may have chosen to stick with a pared down, basic pattern and wait to add pizzazz at the end. The options are so many and their final effects so diverse, but the potential for creating an exceptional fashion is always excitingly present. Sooner or later, you have to decide which effect you will develop. You might depend on ideas to come to you during the construction process, confident that the perfect finishing touch will suggest itself. On the other hand, once you're finished stitching, you might need some renewed creative stimulation. This is precisely when your inspiration bulletin board, scrapbook, or the designer blouses in this book can be very helpful—to encourage you to consider all the options.

Hang up the finished garment where you can see it and visualize different effects as you think about all the decorative possibilities. For example, the simplest addition, such as interesting buttons, decorative appliqué, or detachable fashion features, can transform your garment from ordinary to outstanding. Built-in design features require a bit of pre-planning, such as the custom lace capelet on page 130, pulled thread work on page 66, and refashioned scarf on page 124. But many of the blouses in this book demonstrate a post-construction approach to fashion flair, through the addition of decorative elements after the garment is finished, such as the tatted clover details on page 92, the reversible collar on page 61, and the mitered braid accent on page 53.

As you can see, opportunities for adding your personal design signature to a blouse or shirt are abundant, whether you stitch them into the design right from the beginning or top off the look at the end. Remember that blouse styles are also companion garments and wonderful foundations for accessories; therefore, they can link up with a dramatic partner for yet another look that's full of pizzazz. For example, you may have done some exquisite decorative embroidery on a shirt yoke that really makes the garment special when you wear it by itself over a skirt or slacks. However, you can also wear it under a sweater or jacket, for double wearing duty and even more wardrobe versatility.

BE PREPARED FOR EMERGENCY

The real world being what it is, there are times when things don't go well in the sewing room. In spite of your dedicated preplanning, your efficient sewing technique, and all the good ideas in the world, some garments will not stick with the plan and they defy your attempts to finish them. This fact of life—that sewing disaster is always poised, ready to strike—is especially distressing when your time to sew is so

A Stitch in Time

If a sewing accident happens, take a breather and get away from the problem for a while—take a walk, have a cup of tea, or call it a night. When you come back to it, you'll be better able to assess the damage and come up with a creative fix.

limited in the first place. You might ask yourself, "Why do I bother to sew at all? I can sell all my fabric and purchase a mighty fine ready-to-wear wardrobe."

Sewers rarely do this, however, because of their passion for working with fabric, which always triumphs over any catastrophe. So, when something goes wrong, don't close up the machine and stick on a "For Sale" sign. Instead, trust your ability to recover and follow your personal emergency plan for dealing with disaster. First, remove yourself from the situation. Put the offending project aside, turn off the machine, and leave the area. Go for a walk, make a cup of tea, or have a good cry. In just a few minutes or overnight, you'll recover from the shock effect and be able to figure out how to repair the damage.

Sewing emergencies come in many forms and degrees of seriousness, from pretreating problems and cutting mishaps to stitching hazards and fitting faux pas. Nearly every one of them can be fixed, in some fashion, once you are ready to devise the solution. Some remedies can be as simple as recutting a pattern piece, ripping out a seam and restitching it, or looking for a complementary fabric scrap to make a patch. Others, however, are more difficult and may not succeed. A serious fitting oversight may require disassembling the gar-

A Stitch in Time

Be creative when repairing damage. You can always think up a way to camouflage an error or make a mishap look like an intentional design decision.

ment and starting over. In this case, a recycling effort may be the best solution, in which a dress becomes a blouse or a shirt is salvaged for its collar and cuffs to use on another garment. In fact, recycling a problem garment or disposing of it altogether may be the most therapeutic emergency measure of all. If you cut up or toss out a sewing accident, at least you won't be stuck with an unwearable item and you can start again on something fresh.

Fortunately, blouses provide an extra measure of emergency protection because they can be worn under another garment. If you have to unexpectedly mend a hole or work around some unavoidable fabric flaws, you can easily and successfully disguise such problems with a sweater, vest, jacket, scarf, or attention-getting jewelry. You'll still be able to get good wear out of the item and observers will never notice anything wrong, unless you point it out. Like your other sewing accessories, camouflage is a valuable technical tool, so be brave and use it to rescue your stitching casualties.

A Stitch in Time

When using printed fabrics that require pattern-matching, cut button bands on the bias or out of a complementary solid to eliminate the need to match prints at center front.

You can also save the day with your own creativity. Fix-it measures often become interesting details in their own right, and you may use them again even when no accident has occurred. Unless the designer mentioned it, you would never know that the button loops at the neckline of the blouse on page 120 actually are a method of dealing with a too-small neck opening. Because she had no extra fabric to cut a new neck facing, the designer had to rely on her own ingenuity or give up on the garment. As it turned out, she decided the repair feature was more interesting and attractive than the standard slit at center back, and she will use these neckline loops again, intentionally. Think how you, too, can save the day with a problem-solving technique that becomes an innovative design feature. You will be the only one who knows its disastrous origins.

Common Blouse-Fitting Challenges

The following fitting problems can be remedied in a variety of ways, depending on how much alteration is needed and your preferred method of making adjustments. Refer to a fitting book or video, or sign up for a fitting class that will help you create your own master pattern for a perfectly-fitting garment every time.

Shoulder seams fall to back

Can be caused by exercise-developed back muscles or the naturally changing contours of the upper back over time. If the needed alteration is minor, a small amount can be added to the back at the shoulder seam and an equal amount subtracted from the front. May require an upper back alteration to add fabric in this area without changing armhole, shoulder, or neckline. Patterns with forward shoulders or yoke construction often eliminate this problem.

Gapping neckline

Can be caused by wrong bodice size, too-large neckline opening, or the absence of a bust dart, which will result in pulling the neckline out of shape. Remedies include checking body measurements to ensure correct pattern size, addition or repositioning of bust dart, drafting smaller or slightly curved neck opening.

Too-tight neckline

Can be caused by broad or curved back, full front figure, or forward head position (common in this computer age). Adjustments include enlarging neckline opening a bit, dropping front neckline, and making back or bust alterations. Scoop neck and V-neck styles can eliminate the problem.

Excess fabric in back

A baggy look, with vertical wrinkles in back, is typically due to a narrow back. This can be eliminated by alterations that reduce width in back.

Tight fabric in back

Straining fabric, with horizontal wrinkles across the back, and sleeves that rip out of armholes at the back are due to a broad back. Upper back or full back alterations will add needed width.

Sloping shoulders

The addition of shoulder pads or a shoulder seam alteration will adjust for sloping shoulders. Raglan and dolman sleeves are not recommended for this figure characteristic, unless shoulder pads are used.

Broad and square shoulders

Indicated by fabric pulling and straining at shoulder and armhole area. May require lengthening shoulder seam or adding to armhole height. Raglan and dolman sleeves are well-suited to this figure characteristic.

Front darts in wrong place

Ill-fitting bodice may be due to wrong position of bust point or bust darts. Corrections include moving bust point, moving bust darts or changing their angle, and making alterations to add or subtract width and/or length of bodice front.

Hollow chest

Indicated by excess fabric at front armhole and shoulder area. May require upper chest alteration to reduce width and/or length, shoulder length alteration, or slight padding in area to fill in depression. Some brands of pattern are cut smaller than others in this area.

Incorrect sleeve length

An obvious problem that is easily corrected by lengthening or shortening at indicated lines on sleeve pattern piece. Check arm measurements before cutting sleeves to avoid problem.

Improper sleeve fit at armhole

Too baggy or too tight a fit can be caused by too much or not enough ease, incorrect sleeve cap height, or thin or heavy upper arms. Adjustments include adding or subtracting width to upper sleeve, altering sleeve cap height, or correcting placement of sleeve in armhole, which may have been affected by other shoulder alterations that change position of shoulder point.

THE BLOUSES

The designers of all the blouses in this final section were faced with the same creative challenges as you. They pulled out their favorite patterns and wondered what new spin they could put on them this time around. You will recognize many of the standard blouse styles that form the foundations for all of these beautiful fashions. Simple pullovers, big shirts and tunics, classic button-down shirts, western shirts, cinched-in weskits, and camp shirts-all the basic silhouettes you're familiar with and yet can make such different fashion statements depending on the creative approach you take.

The step-by-step instructions and Plan for the Week guidelines that accompany these blouses show exactly how the designers transformed basic patterns into exciting new wearables-in the limited time they had available to sew. You can do the same thing! Just start with a good idea, choose a simple pattern to work with, and break down the construction into daily tasks that guarantee you'll have a fantastic new addition to your wardrobe by the end of a weekend.

Midnight Mystery

DESIGNER
M. Luanne Carson

This celestial-looking pullover features an overlaid galaxy of manipulated fabric and textured stitching. The simple decorative effects are combined with contrasting material to create out-of-this-world appeal.

Design details

The designer made the blouse straight from a pattern. However, she created a decorative front overlay that was stitched into the blouse shoulder and side seams. For the overlay, she poked self-fabric through the holes of a grid in a random pattern to create "poufs" and then flattened the poufs with machine stitching in decorative arrangements.

Materials and supplies

■ Pattern for basic long-sleeved pullover

■ Fabric of choice, plus ½ yard (.5 m) for front overlay

■ Coordinating print fabric, for neckline and overlay binding

■ Coordinating solid fabric, to be inserted underneath overlay

■ Lightweight fusible interfacing

■ Decorative thread in solid or variegated color

■ Some type of heat-resistant grid with open holes, such as large-holed colander or roasting pan meat rack

■ Notions required by pattern

Construction details

1. Determine the overlay's approximate size by holding the front pattern piece up to your figure and eyeball the overlay placement.

2. Cut a rectangle of self-fabric larger than the pattern piece, at least one-quarter to one-third larger in both width and length. The extra dimensions will be taken up by the fabric manipulation.

3. Cut another rectangle of the same size out of the interfacing.

4. Finish the lower raw edge of the fashion fabric rectangle

with a binding of the coordinating print: Cut a strip equal to the length of the rectangle and press under one long edge; stitch unpressed edge of binding to lower edge of fashion fabric rectangle; press seam toward binding; turn binding to inside and stitch pressed edge in place.

5. With the overlay's wrong side up, poke the fabric down through the holes of your grid device in a random pattern. Poke through a generous amount, about ¾-1¼" (2-3 cm).

6. With fabric still poked through grid, place fusible interfacing over the work area and lightly heat tack in place with iron.

7. Shift fabric to an adjoining section and repeat until you have manipulated the entire rectangle as desired. Note that the edges of the rectangle will be irregular, which will allow the overlay to attractively cascade across the blouse front.

8. Trim off excess interfacing and fuse more firmly in place over entire rectangle.

9. Working on the right side of the rectangle, stitch down the folds and creases that are created by the poking in a decorative manner. Stitch in a sparse or dense manner, as desired.

10. Fold a wide strip of coordinating solid in half and hand stitch invisibly to wrong side of overlay's shaped lower edge. This strip highlights the overlay, creates depth and texture, and acts as a transition between the overlay and the remaining blouse front.

11. Arrange overlay on top of blouse front piece to determine best placement and pin in place. Trim outside edges of overlay even with blouse front and baste together. From this point, you will treat the front and overlay as one piece.

12. Assemble blouse, according to pattern instructions.

13. Bind neckline edge with a bias strip of the coordinating print fabric.

14. Bind sleeve hems with coordinating solid fabric.

Tips from the designer

■ The decorative topstitching on the overlay will add weight and body to the fabric, so you might want to stitch sparingly on a drapey fabric or more densely on a crisp fabric. Too much decorative stitching on a lightweight fabric may create an unwanted stiff effect.

■ The manipulated and stitched overlay will add significant weight to the blouse front and may pull the completed blouse too far forward on your figure. To remedy this, I encased a weight chain in the back neckline only, inside the bias binding. As a result, the garment sets properly on the figure in an unobtrusive manner.

■ Consider some alternative effects with a sheer fabric overlaid over a dark print, or a solid-colored overlay contrasted with a different solid for the blouse body. There are lots of creative options here!

■ Note how different the neckline and overlay bindings look, even though they were cut from the same fabric. The overlay is bound with a strip cut on the lengthwise grain to form a design of repeating squares, but the neckline binding was cut on the bias to form a triangle design.

TO BEGIN THE DECORATIVE EFFECT ON THE FRONT OVERLAY, THE DESIGNER POKED FABRIC RANDOMLY THROUGH THE LARGE HOLES OF A ROASTING PAN MEAT RACK. ANY HEAT-RESISTANT GRID, SUCH AS A LARGE-HOLE COLANDER, WILL WORK. THE PUFFS OF FABRIC THAT ARE POKED THROUGH THE GRID ARE THEN STITCHED DOWN IN A RANDOM MANNER TO CREATE THE DECORATIVE EFFECT ON THE FRONT OVERLAY.

PLAN FOR THE WEEK

Monday

Tuesday

Wednesday

Thursday
Pretreat fabrics.

Friday
Cut out blouse pieces, mark, and interface appropriate pieces; determine overlay size.

Saturday
Cut and bind fabric for overlay; manipulate and stitch overlay; arrange completed overlay on blouse front.

Sunday
Complete blouse assembly; bind neckline edge and sleeve hem; hem blouse.

Catwoman Top
DESIGNER
M. Luanne Carson

Make sewing lots of fun with this simple T-shirt that makes use of graphic piecing, braid trim, and sleeve hem variations.

Design details

The designer split the pattern into quadrants and then cut each quadrant out of different fabrics. She inserted folded bands of contrasting red and black fabric into the front seams, to heighten the graphic effect.

Materials and supplies

■ Pattern for simple pullover, preferably one without an armhole seam

■ Four different fabrics: one blouse length of two fabrics (red, textured white) and ½ yard (.5 m) for remaining two fabrics (Catwoman print, solid black)

■ 1 yard (.95 m) braid or ribbon trim

■ Notions required by pattern

Construction details

1. Slash front and back pattern pieces apart horizontally and vertically, as desired, and add seam allowances to all slashed edges. If you don't want to cut apart the original pattern, trace the pattern pieces and slash apart the traced versions.

2. Use the slashed-apart pattern pieces to cut out the various fabrics, making sure you correctly cut pieces for back and front.

3. Assemble the blouse, inserting folded strips of contrast fabric into seams, as desired. Stitch traditional seams on the inside, or serge seams on the outside with contrasting thread, as desired.

4. Apply mitered braid or ribbon trim to blouse front. See Figure 1. Topstitch in place.

5. Finish neckline and sleeve hems, as desired.

Tips from the designer

■ You can divide any pattern into smaller, pieced components and put the garment together like a jigsaw puzzle. Just remember to add seam allowances to any slashed edges.

■ Let the fabric suggest interesting seam and stitch treatments. For example, on the blouse shown here, I hemmed the Catwoman print sleeve in the traditional turned-under fashion. However, for the opposite sleeve, I decided to serge on top of the hem edge. I thought the white might look too plain next to the cat print, and the black edge seemed just the right touch.

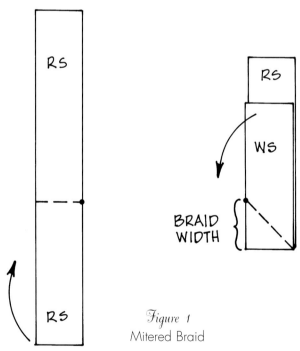

Figure 1
Mitered Braid

To miter the braid trim, mark the outside point of the miter and fold the braid at that point, right sides together (left). On the braid edge opposite of the marked outside point, measure up from the fold the width of the braid and make a mark; chalk a diagonal line connecting the two points (right). Stitch along the diagonal line and press braid open.

Plan for the Week

Monday

∽∽∽∽

Tuesday

∽∽∽∽

Wednesday

∽∽∽∽

Thursday

Pretreat fabrics; slash pattern pieces.

Friday

Cut out blouse, mark, and interface appropriate pieces; assemble blouse.

Saturday

Make and apply mitered braid.

Sunday

Finish sleeve hems and neckline; hem.

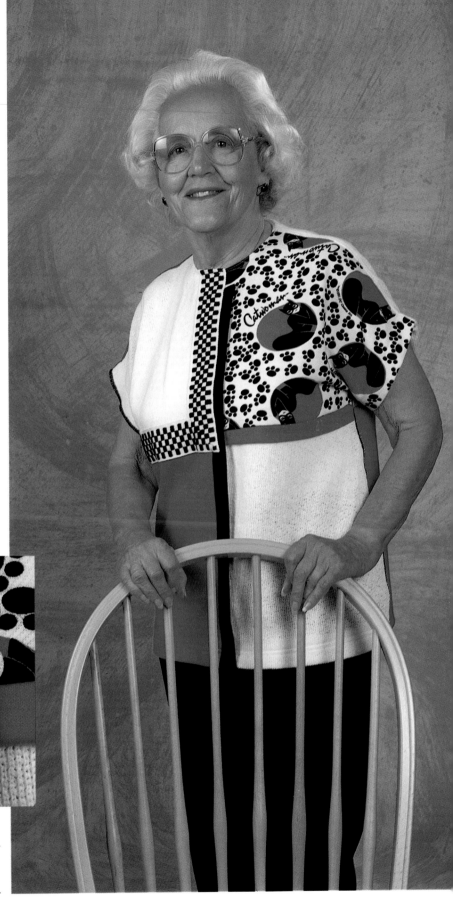

DECORATIVE BRAID IS MITERED TO FORM A NEAT CORNER ON THE FRONT OF THIS PULLOVER BLOUSE.

Fall Flower Garden

DESIGNER

Karen M. Bennett

Wear the seasonal colors of autumn around your neck, with the beautiful russet tones of this silk-embroidered and beaded collar.

Materials and supplies

- Pattern for weskit or blouse, preferably one with a generous collar area

- Fabric of choice

- Assorted sizes of silk ribbon, in colors that coordinate with blouse and skirt fabric

- Glass beads in a coordinating color

- Nylon thread, to sew on beads

- Embroidery hoop

- Chenille needles, size 18-24, for ribbon embroidery

- Beading needle

- Notions required by pattern

Construction details

1. Cut out blouse pattern, excluding collar.

2. Trace collar shape onto a fabric rectangle that is cut a bit larger than collar pattern.

3. Place fabric rectangle in embroidery hoop and begin silk ribbon embroidery, starting with vine. Add flowers in a random design, until desired effect is achieved.

4. Accent embroidery design with beads.

5. Carefully press wrong side of embroidered fabric, to remove any wrinkles.

6. Cut out collar pattern.

7. Assemble garment, according to pattern instructions.

Tips from the designer

- Remember that flowers grow randomly, not in orderly rows. To achieve a natural appearance, place a meandering vine with a variety of flowers weaving around it. Accent the vine by placing beads to act as highlights, or sources of light throughout the piece.

- I keep a small tomato pincushion handy with at least six needles threaded with different colors. Then, I can place flowers where I need them when I see a "hole" in the design.

- Nature is full of contrasts, so have fun and experiment with light and dark color combinations. You will be surprised how light colors can add sparkle to a dark piece.

- Always iron the silk ribbon before stitching! It really shows if you don't.

Plan for the Week

Monday

❧❧❧

Tuesday
Pretreat fabric.

Wednesday
Cut out blouse, mark, and interface appropriate pieces; begin embroidery.

Thursday
Continue embroidery.

Friday
Complete embroidery.

Saturday
Add beadwork accents; begin blouse assembly.

Sunday
Complete blouse assembly; make buttonholes and sew on buttons.

For more information about silk ribbon embroidery:
Montano, Judith Baker. *The Art of Silk Ribbon Embroidery.* Lafayette, California: C&T Publishing, 1993.

Fabulous Faux Front

DESIGNER
Joyce Baldwin

Make the most of your limited sewing time with a quick-to-make dickey that's really an abbreviated blouse. With pretty embroidered trim, you can dress up a sweater, jacket, or any other neckline.

Design details

The designer used a button-front blouse pattern with a basic convertible collar, which has a straight or nearly straight neck edge. Any other collar style that fits close to the base of the neck, such as a Peter Pan, is also suitable. Before cutting out the dickey, analyze the neckline styles of the garments you intend to wear on top. The finished edges of the dickey should extend 4-8" (10-20.5 cm) beyond the garment's neck edge so it will stay tucked underneath.

Materials and supplies

- Blouse pattern of choice, preferably one with a closely-fitted neck area

- Approximately ¾ yard (.7 m) of eyelet lace, broderie edging, or embroidered trim in a 4½-5" (11.5-12.5 cm) width

- Cotton lawn fabric to match eyelet lace

- Lightweight interfacing, if not creating a self-fabric interfacing

- Tracing paper or pattern paper

- Notions required by pattern

Construction details

1. Trace collar piece from your selected blouse pattern, eliminating seam allowances from ends and outer edge. If the collar is cut on the fold, flip piece over and continue tracing, to create a full collar pattern. Alternatively, enlarge and trace collar pattern shown in Figure 1 and flip over to create a full pattern.

2. Establish an angled miter line of approximately 45 degrees, extending from outer corner to neck edge. See Figure 1.

3. To create a self-fabric interfacing, trace a mirror image of the front facing and tape to the front facing edge, as shown in Figure 2.

4. Cut out dickey front and back.

5. Lay collar pattern on top of eyelet lace, with finished edge of lace on collar's outer edge. Shift pattern until collar points

are on top of identical eyelet locations, so lace design will be symmetrical. You may need to slightly alter the collar pattern's shape, to achieve symmetry at the collar points, but do not change the size or shape of the neckline edge.

6. When you are satisfied that the eyelet lace design or scallop shape will be symmetrical, fold ends of the lace, right sides together, and pin along the miter line. See detail photo on next page. Spread pinned lace out flat on a table and place the collar pattern on top, to check once more for symmetrical design.

7. Stitch along miter line and stitch again 1/16" (1.6 mm) away. Trim excess fabric 1/8" (3 mm) from second line of stitching and finish raw edges with a narrow zigzag. Press mitered seam to one side.

8. Pin collar pattern to mitered lace and trim away excess fabric along the unfinished neck edge.

9. On dickey fronts, press under self-interfacing along fold-line, wrong sides together.

10. Sew fronts to back at shoulder seams. Use French or flat-felled seams (see page 86) for a finished appearance, or stitch in traditional seams, finish raw edges, and press open.

11. Pin and baste collar to right side of neck edge.

12. Turn facing along foldline, right sides together, and stitch across the V-shaped area at lower center front.

13. Cut a self-fabric bias strip, 1½" (4 cm) wide and a bit longer than the neckline seam measurement. Pin and baste bias strip on top of collar and neck edge, with ends extend-

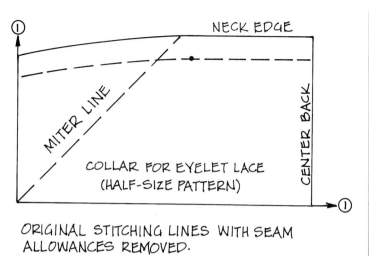

NECK EDGE

MITER LINE

CENTER BACK

COLLAR FOR EYELET LACE
(HALF-SIZE PATTERN)

ORIGINAL STITCHING LINES WITH SEAM
ALLOWANCES REMOVED.

Figure 1

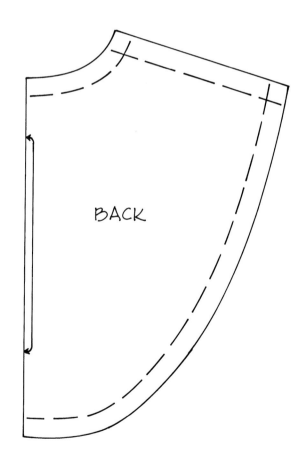

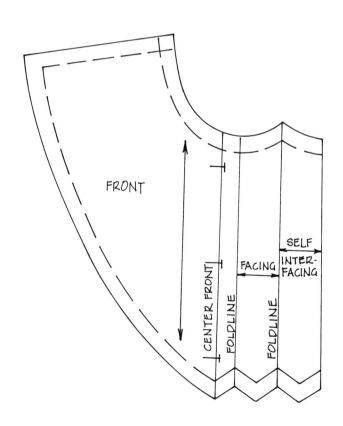

FRONT

CENTER FRONT

FOLDLINE

FACING

FOLDLINE

SELF

INTER-
FACING

Figure 2

BACK

Figure 3

ing ½" (1.25 cm) into facing. Stitch neck seam, trim, and clip curves.

14. Turn bias strip and front facing to inside of dickey and press. Measured from neck seam, bias strip should be approximately ½" (1.25 cm) wide, plus ¼" (6 mm) for turning under. Trim off any excess.

15. Turn under ¼" (6 mm) of raw edge and slipstitch or topstitch to enclose neck seam.

16. Hem dickey, make buttonholes, and sew on buttons.

Tips from the designer

Even though you may remember wearing a dickey when it was in style years ago, it's really an accessory that deserves to stay around permanently. This abbreviated blouse has so many advantages:

■ Once you have worked out the how-to, it can be made in one evening.

■ You have the opportunity to try out new collar styles, with a minimal investment in materials. You can splurge on a small quantity of exquisite fabric!

■ A dickey pattern made up in several collar styles and fabrics is a great wardrobe extender.

■ If you use eyelet lace or other embroidered trim, you can create the appearance of heirloom sewing, but in a fraction of the time.

■ A dickey fills in lower necklines on garments and helps cover a long neck or less than youthful skin. It can also be used to place a flattering color close to the face.

■ There's no waste! You can use remnants from other sewing projects.

■ It's so versatile. Lengthen to below the waistline as a filler for jackets.

Plan for the Week

Monday

Tuesday

Wednesday

Thursday
Pretreat fabric.

Friday
Modify pattern; cut out dickey, mark, and interface appropriate pieces.

Saturday
Make eyelet collar; assemble front and back.

Sunday
Attach collar; finish neckline; make buttonholes and sew on buttons.

Flipped-Out Top
DESIGNER
Sonia A. Huber

Show off this original collar, and then flip it over for a totally different presentation. It's easy, fun, and provides two "canvases" for your self-expression.

Design details

The designer started with a simple jewel-neck shell pattern and used the front pattern piece to draft the five-panel detachable collar that buttons at the shoulder seams.

Materials and supplies

- Pattern for simple jewel-neck shell

- Fabric of choice, for shell

- Six assorted fabrics for reversible collar sections, approximately ¼ yard (.25 m) of each

- 12" (30.5 cm) grosgrain ribbon, 1" (2.5 cm) wide, for shell construction

- 24" (61 cm) grosgrain or satin ribbon, 1" (2.5 cm) wide, for "epaulets"

- Bias tape

- Tracing paper

- Marking pen

- Scissors

- Ruler

- Notions required by pattern

Construction details

1. Assemble shell, according to pattern instructions.

2. Stabilize shoulders by stitching a length of grosgrain ribbon down the center of the shoulder seams on the inside.

3. Draft the five-panel collar as follows: Place tracing paper over front pattern piece and trace outline. Draw a diagonal line from front sleeve notch to waistline mark at center front. See Figure 1. Draw a vertical line down from point A cutting line to point B. Draw another vertical line down from point C cutting line to point D, just touching the armhole. Divide the distance between C and A, and place a dot at that point on cutting line; label as point E. Draw a vertical line down from point E to point F.

4. Cut the panel pieces apart, remembering to indicate that panel #1 is to be placed on the fold. On another piece of tracing paper, trace each panel separately, adding desired seam allowances on three edges (two edges on panel #1).

5. Cut panel sections from assorted fabrics. Select fabrics that are lightweight enough so the completed collar does not pull the shoulders forward.

6. Place sections right sides together and stitch, leaving neck edges open. Clip corners, trim, turn right side out, and press.

7. Apply ready-made bias tape or a self-fabric bias edging to neckline edge of center panel.

8. Lay the center panel, a middle panel, and a short outside panel side by side.

9. Cut four epaulets from the grosgrain or satin ribbon to equal the width of the three panels, plus a small amount to turn under.

10. Sandwich three panels between two of the ribbon epaulets, raw panel edges even with top edge of the ribbon. Edgestitch along the bottom of the epaulets. Trim a small amount off the raw panel edges, then edgestitch along the epaulet's top edge.

11. Repeat for other half of collar.

12. Make two buttonholes in the epaulets, about 1" (2.5 cm) in from each end.

"I have become very interested in designing garments that have movement of their own. This collar began with just a single panel, but then I wondered: Why not more than one? Why not make it reversible?"

61

13. Lay the completed collar flat and tack the edges of the five panels together with small hand stitches, at about 1" (2.5 cm) intervals from the epaulets down the front about 5" (12.5 cm). This will keep the collar together as a unit and prevent the panels from flapping around.

14. Lay the collar on the assembled shell, and center the buttonholes on the shoulder seamline.

15. Mark button placement and sew buttons on.

TIPS FROM THE DESIGNER

■ Before assembling the collar panels, make sure fabrics don't show through from the reverse side. And select collar fabrics that are lightweight enough to prevent pulling the shoulders forward.

■ Faux leather is a great alternative for the epaulets. It provides a nice look and can be trimmed close to the edges. Remember to use a sharp needle. If you use satin ribbon, you may need to stabilize it with interfacing.

■ If the sleeve cap of a blouse pattern is high and difficult to ease into the armhole, just make two or more small pleats at the sleeve head.

Plan for the Week

Monday

Tuesday

Wednesday

Thursday
Pretreat fabrics; draft five-panel collar pattern.

Friday
Cut out blouse, mark, and interface appropriate pieces.

Saturday
Assemble blouse; cut out pieces for collar.

Sunday
Assemble five-panel collar; make buttonholes and sew on buttons; attach collar to blouse.

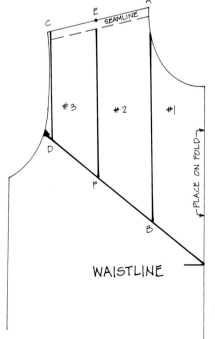

WAISTLINE

Figure 1

White Linen

DESIGNER
Sally Hickerson

This crisp, white blouse is far from plain-looking, with its asymmetrical pintucked pattern across the front opening. With just a little advance planning, you can tuck any piece, in any direction, for a subtle expression of style.

Design details

■ The designer started with a classic blouse pattern, but added pintucking to the yoke, cuffs, and fronts. She completed the tucking on rectangles of the linen fabric before cutting out the yoke and cuff pattern pieces. She did not use cording inside the tucks, and the result is a very subtle pattern, rather than a high relief effect.

■ For the fronts, she tucked the left side first. She then folded the right front pattern piece under along the front foldline and laid it down over the pintucked left, to see where the left and right tucks would have to meet. Small marks on the right front pattern piece indicated where the lines of pintucking needed to cross the foldline. A little extra fabric, around all edges of the front pieces, provided enough allowance for the tucking.

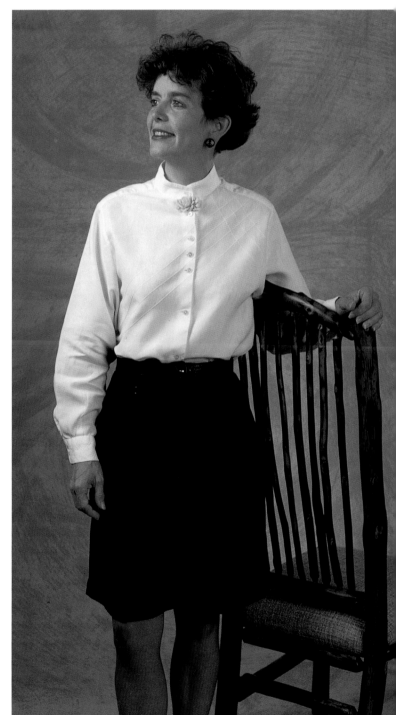

Patchwork Blues
DESIGNER
Mary Russell

Jazz up a simple T-shirt pattern with this fun patchwork palette and show off some favorite fabric swatches at the same time.

Materials and supplies

■ Pattern for simple pullover or T-shirt, preferably one with only two pattern pieces (front and back)

■ Assorted fabrics of choice

■ Lining fabric of choice

■ Coordinating cotton ribbing

■ Fabric markers

■ Cardboard or sheet plastic

■ Notions required by pattern

Tips from the designer

■ With this patchwork approach to creating custom yardage, you can be as subtle or as outrageous as you like. Tone it down, in a monochrome effect, or let the colors sing! You can even embellish the pieced material with beads, embroidery, and other decorative touches.

Construction details

1. Make a cardboard or plastic template of the pattern shown here. With the fabric marker, trace around the template onto the back of various fabrics.

2. Cut out 50-60 patterns and stitch together on the diagonal, in various arrangements to make 25-30 squares.

3. Arrange the patchwork squares on top of the blouse front and back pattern pieces until you are satisfied with the arrangement. Sew the blocks together, with ¼" (6 mm) seam allowances, to form enough yardage for that area. This will probably be an irregular shape.

4. Add other strips and larger pieces of fabric to cover the entire pattern. Piece together, to form yardage.

5. Cut the front and back pattern pieces from your pieced yardage.

6. Cut front and back pieces from lining fabric.

7. Assemble and line blouse, leaving neckline and hem unfinished.

8. Stitch cotton ribbing to neck edge and hem.

Plan for the Week

Monday
〰〰〰

Tuesday
〰〰〰

Wednesday
〰〰〰

Thursday
Make pattern template and cut out patterns.

Friday
Stitch patchwork squares; begin piecing yardage.

Saturday
Finish piecing yardage; cut out blouse front and back; cut out lining.

Sunday
Assemble and line blouse; attach ribbing at neck edge and hem.

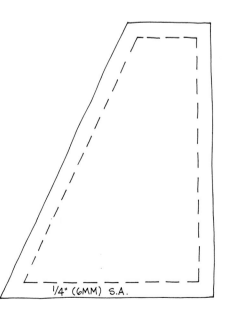

1/4" (6MM) S.A.

PATCHWORK PATTERN

Heirloom Camp Shirt
DESIGNER
Joyce Baldwin

The most basic of blouse styles, such as the camp shirt, can be transformed into a special wardrobe collectible with some decorative pulled thread details-such as this ladder hemstitching technique.

Design details

The designer started with a basic camp shirt pattern that features a curved front/neckline self-facing that is cut in one with the bodice. She changed the front facing to a band, and replaced the neckline facing with a bias strip to cover and finish the neckline seam on the inside. Because the collar is a single thickness of fabric, she also added a hem allowance to the outer edges that was turned up and secured by the hemstitching.

Materials and supplies

- Shirt pattern of choice

- Handkerchief linen fabric of choice (see designer tip on page 68)

- Lightweight woven sew-in interfacing, for front band

- Thread to match fabric, and quilting thread for hemstitching

- Embroidery hoop (optional, to hold fabric taut while hemstitching)

- Entredeux trim or faggoting (optional, to apply by machine instead of hemstitching by hand)

- Notions required by pattern

"I got the idea for this decorative hemstitching from my mother, who has won awards for her complex drawn thread tablecloths, which take hundreds of hours to complete. I don't have that kind of time right now, so I chose the simplest form to ornament the shirt."

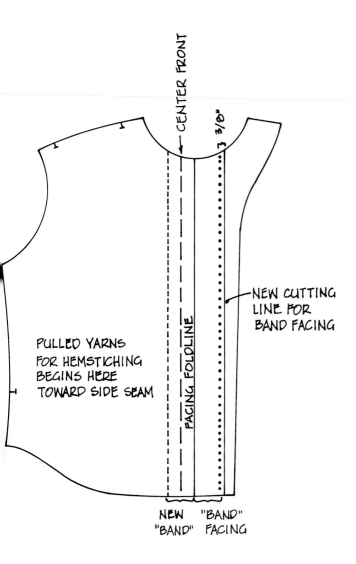

PULLED YARNS
FOR HEMSTICHING
BEGINS HERE
TOWARD SIDE SEAM

CENTER FRONT

3/8"

FACING FOLDLINE

NEW CUTTING
LINE FOR
BAND FACING

NEW "BAND" "BAND" FACING

Figure 1

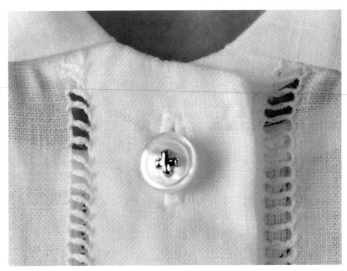

THIS LADDER HEMSTITCHING IS A PRETTY FORM OF DRAWN THREAD OR
PULLED THREAD WORK. FOR A SIMILAR EFFECT, STORE-BOUGHT ENTREDEUX
TRIM OR FAGGOTING COULD BE APPLIED BY MACHINE INSTEAD OF DOING
THE PULLED THREAD WORK BY HAND.

Construction details

1. On front pattern piece, measure distance from center front (CF) to facing foldline. Measure and mark an equal distance from CF toward side seam. This is the point at which you will begin pulling threads for hemstitching, to create the front "band" effect. See Figure 1.

2. To change the shaped front self-facing to a straight fold-back band facing, measure and mark a new cutting line that is the width of the new front band plus 3/8" (1 cm) seam allowance to turn under. See Figure 1.

3. The collar pattern piece may need some alteration, for the hemstitching. The front corners of the collar pattern must form an on-grain right angle, to ease pulling threads. To secure the collar hem with the hemstitching, the seam allowances on the outer edges must be widened to equal the desired hem width, plus 3/8" (1 cm) to turn under. See Figure 2 for collar alterations.

4. Omit the back neckline facing piece. To finish the neckline edge after the collar has been basted in place, stitch a self-fabric bias strip to the neckline seam; turn to the inside and topstitch or blind-stitch in place on the inside.

5. The lower edge of the sleeve must be an on-grain straight edge for hemstitching. If necessary, straighten the underarm cutting line and seamline.

A DICKEY WITH DECORATIVE COLLAR IS A FAST WAY TO EXPERIMENT WITH
DRAWN THREAD WORK OR CREATE A BEAUTIFUL WARDROBE EXTENDER THAT
CAN BE WORN UNDER JACKETS OR SWEATERS.

Tips from the designer

■ Some fabrics are better than others for pulled thread work.
Fabric for hemstitching should have few slubs or other texture,
and should be evenly woven of strong threads that can be
easily pulled without breaking. It's definitely worth buying
⅛ yard (.15 m) of fabric to test thread strength and practice
your hemstitching technique. Check your local library or
sewing resource center for books and information sheets on
hemstitching.

■ If hemstitching by hand is not your cup of tea, consider the
many beautiful heirloom sewing trims that can be attached by
machine, including faggoting and entredeux. A bonus of
using purchased trim is that it can be applied on the bias,
which means your fabric options are not quite as limited.

■ A dickey with hemstitched collar, like the one shown here,
is a fast and perfect way to get the effect and determine if
you like the technique.

Plan for the Week

Monday

Tuesday
Pretreat fabric; modify pattern for hemstitching.

Wednesday
Cut out blouse, mark, and interface appropriate pieces.

Thursday
Pull threads on pockets and front band area.

Friday
Hemstitch pockets; begin blouse assembly.

Saturday
Pull threads on collar and hemstitch; attach collar and finish
back neckline; hemstitch front band.

Sunday
Pull threads on sleeves and hemstitch; insert sleeves into
blouse; hem; make buttonholes and sew on buttons.

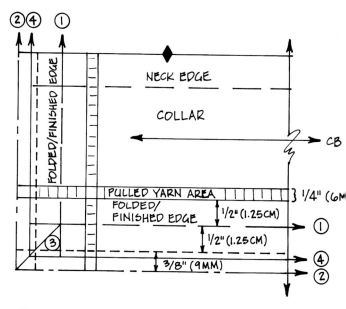

① ORIGINAL STITCHING LINES BECOME
   FOLDED / FINISHED COLLAR EDGES.
② NEW CUTTING LINES.
③ MITERED CORNER.
④ ORIGINAL CUTTING LINES.

Figure 2

Hawaiian Style
DESIGNER
Laurie Cervantes

Update the lines of a traditional Hawaiian shirt pattern for a more contemporary look, and replace the turned hem with a self-fabric band for subtle design contrast.

Design details

The designer started with a vintage 1970s pattern that featured a wide collar, folded front self-facings, tapered waistline, and roomy elbow-length sleeves. She kept the wide collar, noting the current popularity of this "retro" style, but straightened the tapered side seams, shortened the sleeves, and removed a bit of ease at the sleeve cap. She also substituted an interfaced button band for the front opening, while maintaining the self-facing around the neck edge.

Materials and supplies

■ Pattern for traditional Hawaiian shirt

■ Fabric of choice, including matching or contrasting yardage for bands at front opening, sleeve hem, and shirt hem

■ ¼ yard (.25 m) fusible interfacing

■ Notions required by pattern

Construction details

1. To remove some of the sleeve volume, make a ¼" (6 mm) fold in the sleeve pattern piece from shoulder point to hem edge.

2. Make a new shirt front pattern piece to replace the self-facing with interfaced button band, as follows. From the hem edge, trace a new front cutting line ½" (1.25 cm) inside the self-facing foldline up to a point 1" (2.5 cm) below the top buttonhole mark; you will stitch the button band to this front edge in a ¼" (6 mm) seam. Then, draw a line horizontally into the self-facing about 1" (2.5 cm) and gradually taper to the original self-facing cutting line. See Figure 1. Finish the

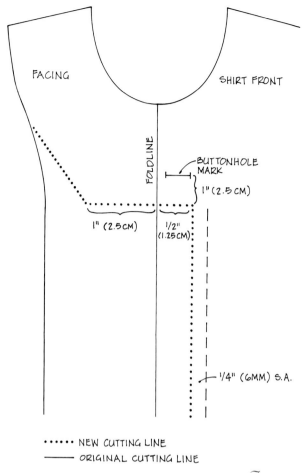

FACING   SHIRT FRONT

FOLDLINE

BUTTONHOLE MARK

1" (2.5 CM)

1" (2.5 CM)   1/2" (1.25 CM)

1/4" (6MM) S.A.

• • • • • NEW CUTTING LINE
———— ORIGINAL CUTTING LINE

Figure 1

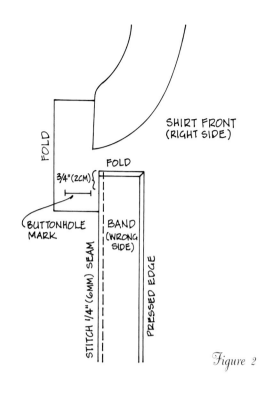

SHIRT FRONT (RIGHT SIDE)

FOLD

FOLD

3/4" (2CM)

BUTTONHOLE MARK

BAND (WRONG SIDE)

STITCH 1/4" (6MM) SEAM

PRESSED EDGE

Figure 2

raw edge of the remaining self-facing, as desired, before stitching the button band to the front edge.

3. Assemble shirt, according to pattern instructions, replacing folded hems and front facing with self-fabric bands, as follows.

4. For the front button and hem bands, cut strips of self-fabric or contrasting fabric 2" (6 mm) wide along the lengthwise grain, to a length equal to the sleeve hem, shirt hem, and front opening edge plus 1/4" (6 mm) seam allowances.

5. Press hem bands in half lengthwise and then press under 1/4" (6 mm) along one edge. Stitch unpressed edge to hem, right sides together; press seam toward band; turn band to

inside and topstitch pressed edge in place.

6. Press front button bands in half lengthwise and then press under 1/4" (6 mm) along one edge.

7. Cut narrow strips of fusible interfacing and apply to wrong side of button bands along unpressed edge, to provide stability for buttonholes and buttons.

8. Fold under 1/4" (6 mm) at top end of button band and stitch unpressed edge of band to front edge, from hem to 3/4" (2 cm) above top buttonhole mark, using 1/4" (6 mm) seams. See Figure 2. Press seam toward band and turn band to outside. See Figure 3.

9. Fold top of band down diagonally, as shown in Figure 4.

10. Turn band to inside of shirt, and topstitch close to seamline along diagonal edge and long edge of band. See Figure 5.

Tips from the designer

■ You can often find old coconut, wood, or bamboo buttons in thrift shops and antique stores. Keep your eyes open for these finds, as they really make a newly made Hawaiian style shirt look genuine.

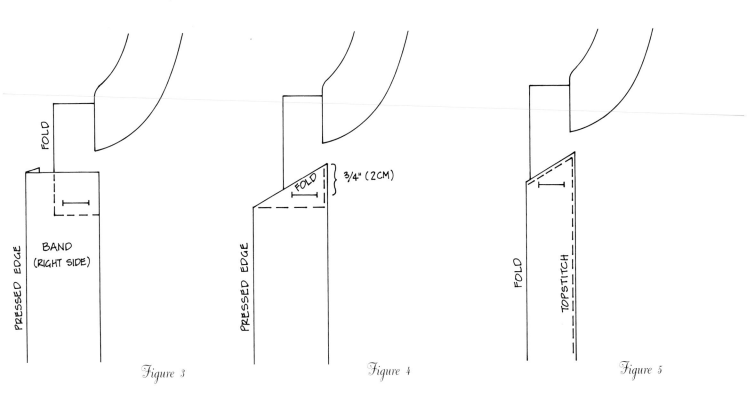

FOLD

PRESSED EDGE

BAND
(RIGHT SIDE)

Figure 3

FOLD

3/4" (2CM)

PRESSED EDGE

Figure 4

FOLD

TOPSTITCH

Figure 5

Alternatives for neckline and front opening.

■ Create different effects by using different prints or solid-colored fabrics for the bands. Depending on how it looks, you could even use the same fabric for the bands, but let the wrong side show.

■ Experiment with various styles for the front opening edges, like I have in my designer sketches. With such simple pattern alterations, the finished shirt can look completely different.

Plan for the Week

Monday

∿∿∿∿

Tuesday

∿∿∿∿

Wednesday
Pretreat fabrics.

Thursday
Modify pattern to reduce sleeve volume and substitute button band for self-facing.

Friday
Cut out blouse, mark, and interface appropriate pieces.

Saturday
Assemble blouse.

Sunday
Apply hem and button bands; make buttonholes and sew on buttons.

Purple Passion
DESIGNER
Mary S. Parker

Make a favorite blouse suddenly new again by turning a standard front opening into a sophisticated concealed placket and then embellish it with tone-on-tone embroidery.

Materials and supplies

- Pattern for blouse with extended front self-facing (front and front facing are one piece)
- Fabric of choice
- Extra pattern tissue or paper
- Removable tape
- Ruler and pencil
- Tear-away stabilizer, for placket embroidery
- Rayon machine embroidery thread
- Notions required by the pattern

Construction details

1. Fold under front facing extension along the foldline and crease with a cool iron. Open up the pattern tissue and cut along the foldline, to separate the facing from the blouse front. See Figure 1.

2. Cut a piece of pattern paper 4" (10 cm) wide and a bit longer than the blouse front. Draw a line down the center, from top to bottom; draw two more lines on either side of and parallel to the first, 1¼" (3 cm) away.

3. Tape the edge of the blouse front pattern along one of the outside lines you just drew, and the inner edge of the cutaway facing along the other line. Your original pattern will now have a 2½" (6.5 cm) insertion. See Figure 2.

4. Fold the taped pattern along lines #1 and #3, so the cut edges of the two original pattern pieces touch each other once again; the insertion will form a pleat underneath. Pin the pattern to hold the pleat temporarily, and trim the insertion's top and bottom edges even with those of the original pattern.

5. While the insertion is still folded under, cut out a left blouse front, remembering to flip the pattern or fabric over so you will have both a left and right front.

6. Open out the altered pattern and cut a right blouse front. Mark lines #1, #2, and #3 with small scissor cuts at the top and bottom edges or tailor tacks.

7. Cut remaining blouse and interfacing pieces, according to pattern instructions. Apply interfacing to the wrong side of the facing extension and finish outer raw edge.

8. To embroider the front placket, fold the right front along line #1, wrong sides together. Press the fold, and iron a narrow strip of tear-away stabilizer to the underside. Complete the embroidery, using rayon thread, and remove the stabilizer. See Figure 3.

9. Fold the underside piece back against itself, right sides together, so lines #1 and #3 are matched and the original facing extension is protruding beyond the blouse front. See Figure 4. Machine baste resulting pleat in place.

10. Fold the facing extension over, on top of the blouse, so it fits snugly around the basted pleat. See Figure 4.

11. Stitch the neck edge through all thicknesses, to secure the pleat. Remove basting and turn right side out, to check that the facing was sufficiently snug around the pleat and that it is now hidden behind the pleat.

12. Complete blouse assembly, making buttonholes in the concealed under layer of the front placket.

This intricate embroidery was actually quite simple to do, using a combination of machine embroidery stitches in three different passes (the central motif was stitched first, followed by a scallop stitch along one side, and then the scallop stitch set on "mirror image" along the other side). Combinations of stitches available on your machine can yield lots of different results.

TIPS FROM THE DESIGNER

■ Improvise pretty and intricate embroidery designs by combining stitches on your machine. In the blouse shown here, I stitched the central motif first and then added two rows of scallop stitch on either side. Just three simple passes on the machine, and the result looks like a very intricate embroidery design.

■ To get even more design mileage out of this concealed placket, make the top buttonhole through all layers of fabric and sew on a small plain button. Then, use several different button covers for a changing wardrobe of finishing touches.

THIS BASIC BLOUSE STYLE WAS ALTERED TO CREATE A COMPLETELY HIDDEN BUTTON PLACKET, SO THE DECORATIVE EMBROIDERY WOULD BE THE HIGHLIGHT.

THIS VERSION OF THE SAME BLOUSE STYLE WAS ALSO ALTERED TO CREATE A HIDDEN BUTTON PLACKET. HOWEVER, A SMALL, PLAIN TOP BUTTON WAS SEWN ON THE OUTSIDE—TO STAND ALONE OR BE EASILY COVERED BY ANY OF THE DECORATIVE BUTTON COVERS SHOWN HERE, FOR DESIGN VERSATILITY.

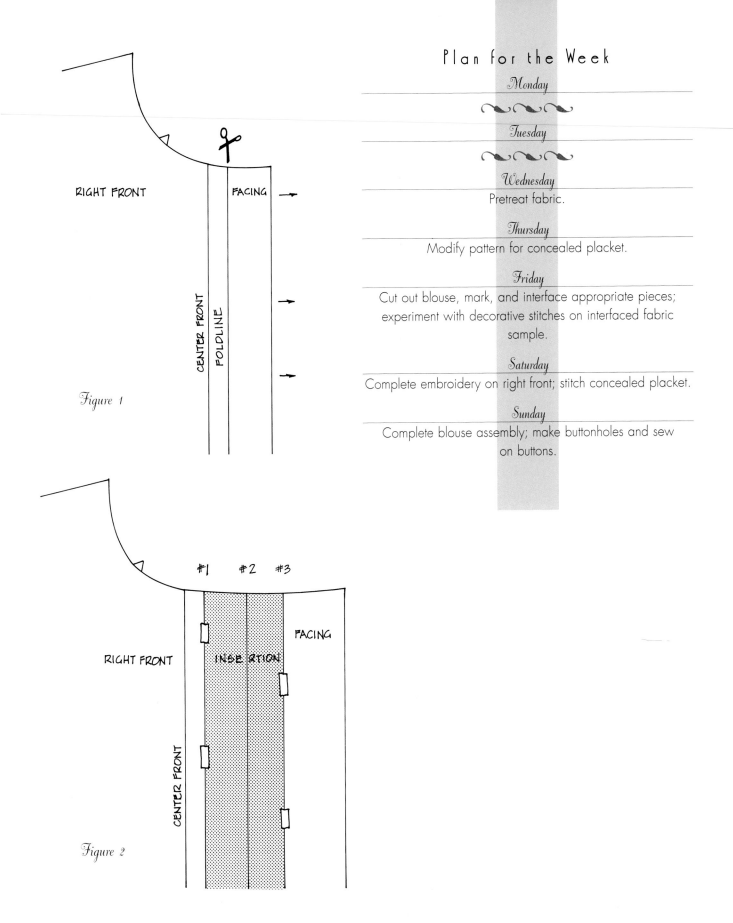

RIGHT FRONT

FACING

CENTER FRONT

FOLDLINE

Figure 1

RIGHT FRONT

FACING

INSERTION

#1   #2   #3

CENTER FRONT

Figure 2

Monday

Tuesday

Wednesday
Pretreat fabric.

Thursday
Modify pattern for concealed placket.

Friday
Cut out blouse, mark, and interface appropriate pieces; experiment with decorative stitches on interfaced fabric sample.

Saturday
Complete embroidery on right front; stitch concealed placket.

Sunday
Complete blouse assembly; make buttonholes and sew on buttons.

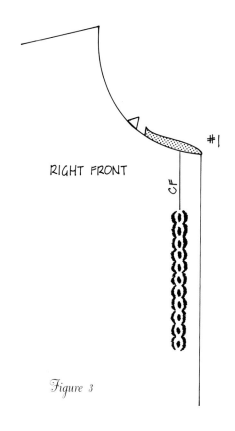

RIGHT FRONT

CF

Figure 3

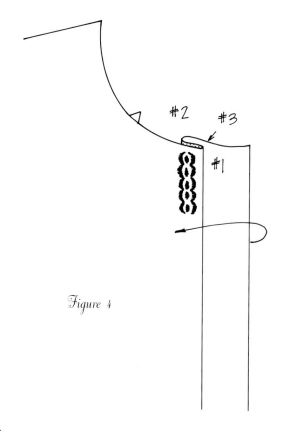

#2   #3

#1

Figure 4

Emerald Classic

DESIGNER
Linda Boyd

Design details

The placement of the top buttonhole in the original pattern created too low an opening for the designer's comfort, but she couldn't just move the buttonhole up, as that would interfere with the curve of the front opening edge. She, therefore, redrew the curve of the blouse front and front facing to accommodate a higher buttonhole. See Figure 1.

Materials and supplies

- Pattern for classic blouse style

- Fabric of choice

- Double needles, size 2.5 or 3.0

- Pintucking sewing machine foot

- Quilting seam guide sewing machine attachment, if available

- 10 yards (9.15 m) gimp cord, optional for pintuck filler

- Notions as required by pattern

Construction details

1. Lay out and cut pattern pieces, cutting only one yoke and no cuffs at this time. Be sure to leave uncut portions of fabric about 5" (12.5 cm) wide and 5" (12.5 cm) longer than normally required to cut a yoke and cuffs.

2. Mark the straight of grain on one uncut piece of fabric, to be used for the pintucked yoke. If you are concerned that a chalk or other mark will not come out of the fabric, lightly press a crease to indicate the grainline.

The rich emerald color of this classic blouse style is well put together with the textured pintucked yoke and cuffs to create a first-class impression.

PINTUCKING OVER GIMP CORD RESULTS IN WELL-DEFINED LINES AND PRO-NOUNCED RELIEF.

3. Insert double needle and thread machine, as recommended in your owner's manual.

4. Thread gimp cord up through needle plate. Refer to owner's manual or check with your sewing machine dealer for information about the proper placement of gimp cord for corded pintucks.

5. Begin stitching along the marked grainline or center of fabric piece. Use a quilting or seam guide to help you space the pintucks equally. In the blouse shown here, pintucks are ¾" (2 cm) apart.

6. Continue stitching pintucks on each side, working from the center out, until the entire fabric piece has been stitched. Press, without flattening pintucks, by placing tucks down on a thick terrycloth towel.

7. Fold the fabric piece in half, in the opposite direction, and press a crease line. This will be the first row of pintucking along the crossgrain of the fabric.

8. Space and stitch pintucks, as above, so they are perpendicular to the first set, working from the center out. Press, as above.

9. Arrange yoke pattern piece on pintucked fabric until tucks are symmetrically positioned, and cut out yoke.

10. Pintuck and cut out cuffs, as you did for the yoke.

11. Assemble blouse, according to pattern instructions.

Tips from the designer

■ I have found that natural fibers work best for pintucking. Polyester and polyester blends want to pucker and pull.

■ Always try out your pintucking on a fabric scrap before stitching on the garment pieces. You need to make sure everything will work right, but making samples also provides the opportunity to experiment with different thread colors and decorative stitches.

■ If you're using a double needle, just be sure that your stitch motif is not too wide, or it may break the needle. Your sewing machine may have a double stitch setting, which keeps the left-right swing of the needle from getting dangerously wide.

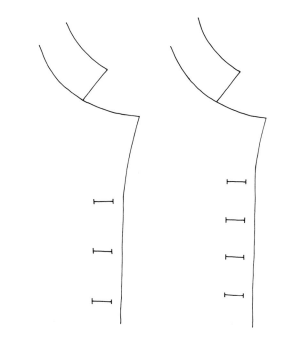

Figure 1

Plan for the Week

Monday

Tuesday

Wednesday
Pretreat fabric.

Thursday
Stitch sampler for pintucking.

Friday
Cut out blouse (except yoke and cuffs), mark, and interface appropriate pieces.

Saturday
Pintuck fabric rectangles for yoke and cuffs; cut out yoke and cuffs; begin blouse assembly.

Sunday
Complete blouse assembly; make buttonholes and sew on buttons.

Marbled Icing

DESIGNER
Mary S. Parker

Piece your small treasures of marbled fabric into a truly distinctive blouse that shows off this fascinating technique. And don't clutter up the marbling with a button front; instead move the opening to the back and decorate the front with a non-functional button trim.

Materials and supplies

■ Favorite blouse pattern, preferably one that is closely fitted, such as a princess style, to reduce the bulk of pieced fabric

■ Fabric samples that add up to approximately 20 percent more yardage than is called for by the pattern

■ Lightweight but stable fabric for under layer, which will show only on the inside; yardage amount as required by blouse pattern

■ Rotary cutter and mat, for cutting marbled fabric strips

■ Decorative cording and buttons, for front "placket" trim, if functional opening is moved to back

■ Functional buttons, if opening is moved to back

Construction details

1. Cut out the under layer, according to pattern layout. Indicate the straight of grain on the middle of each piece, drawing a pencil line from top to bottom.

2. Cut marbled fabrics into strips and then into rectangles. The marbled samples used in the blouse shown here measured approximately 15" (38 cm) wide by 22" (56 cm) long. They were first cut into five strips, 3" (7.5 cm) wide. The strips were then cut into four rectangles, 5½" (14 cm) long. See Figure 1.

3. Reassemble the rectangles, end to end, into attractive strips that are long enough to extend from the top to the bottom of the various under layer pieces. You do not have to sew all the strips at once, or make them all the same length; you will use excess fabric from some of the strips to "fill in"

empty space on other strips.

4. Lay one strip, right side up, on top of an under layer piece, making sure that the long sides of the strip are parallel to the penciled grainline.

5. Place a second strip of the same length on top of the first strip, right sides together, keeping edges aligned with grainline. Pin in place along one long edge and sew in a ¼" (6 mm) seamline through all thicknesses. Press seam open and topstitch both strips ¼" (6 mm) from seamline.

6. Repeat, until the under layer piece is completely covered.

7. Turn assembled piece over, so the under layer is visible. Stitch around the outside of the piece, to secure all edges. Trim off any excess marbled fabric, and set aside for use on other pieces.

8. If you desire the faux front, to emphasize the marbling, be sure to add allowances for a buttoned opening at center back. Couch decorative cording to the blouse front with invisible nylon thread, using a small zigzag stitch, before joining the front to other garment sections.

9. When all the under layer pieces are covered with marbled fabric, complete the blouse, according to pattern instructions.

10. Sew decorative buttons on faux front, if desired.

Tips from the designer

■ You may fall in love with the marbling technique at your first class, but the samples you bring home may not look as expert as you would like. Cutting up the samples to make pieced strips really draws attention to the beautiful technique, not to your beginning level skills.

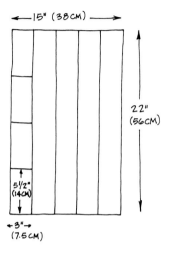

Figure 1

Plan for the Week

Monday

Tuesday

Wednesday
Pretreat fabrics.

Thursday
Cut out and mark under layer.

Friday
Cut marbled strips and reassemble into pleasing arrangements.

Saturday
Complete strip piecing to cover under layer; couch decorative cord to front; begin blouse assembly.

Sunday
Complete blouse assembly; make buttonholes and sew on buttons.

Eyelet Confection
DESIGNER
Joyce Baldwin

Soften the lines of a tailored suit with this feminine eyelet blouse. It's both pretty and so easy to do, with just a few modifications of a standard blouse pattern.

Design and construction details

The designer used a standard blouse pattern with front and back pleated into the yoke, released pleats at the waist, and long cuffed sleeves. To take advantage of the pretty eyelet fabric, she laid out the pattern pieces along the scalloped edge, as shown in Figure 1, after making these minor changes to the pattern:

1. For a short-sleeved blouse, simply shorten sleeves to desired length. For a long-sleeved blouse, omit cuffs and sleeve vents and place sleeve end on scalloped edge of fabric.

2. Modify collar pattern piece as described for the Fabulous Faux Front dickey on page 56.

3. Eliminate facing from center front edge of right front pattern piece. For a pattern with a cut-in-one facing, place the foldline on the indented points of the scallops. For a pattern with a separate facing, place the stitching line on the indented points.

4. Add a self-fabric interfacing to the center front edge of the left front pattern piece, as described for the Fabulous Faux Front dickey on page 56.

5. The right front will have no facing or interfacing. To stabilize and strengthen the buttonhole area, cut small rectangles of organdy ½" (1.25 cm) larger than buttonholes and baste to the wrong side of fabric before making buttonholes.

6. Prepare a single-layer collar with mitered front corners, as described for the Fabulous Faux Front dickey on page 56.

Tips from the designer

■ Before making buttonholes, study the shape and design of the finished eyelet edge. Then, try to balance the buttonhole size and spacing with the eyelet design. Avoid disrupting any

embroidery motifs near the finished outside edge.

■ The right front will have no facing or interfacing, but you still must reinforce the buttonhole area. Small rectangles of organdy work well for this.

THE SCALLOPED EDGES OF READY-MADE EYELET FABRIC MAKE A PERFECT SHAPED FRONT OPENING AND COLLAR. THE DESIGNER POSITIONED THE BUTTONS SO THEY WOULDN'T INTERFERE WITH THE EMBROIDERY MOTIFS, AND LIGHTLY STABILIZED BEHIND THE BUTTONS WITH SMALL RECTANGLES OF ORGANDY.

Plan for the Week

Monday

Tuesday

Wednesday
Pretreat fabric.

Thursday
Modify pattern to take advantage of eyelet edge.

Friday
Lay out, cut, and mark blouse.

Saturday
Begin blouse assembly; prepare collar.

Sunday
Complete blouse assembly; make buttonholes and sew on buttons; hem.

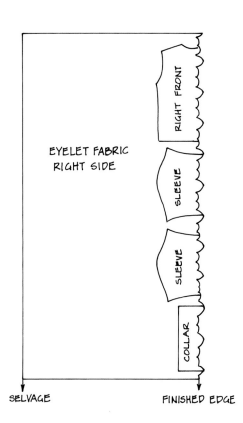

EYELET FABRIC
RIGHT SIDE

RIGHT FRONT

SLEEVE

SLEEVE

COLLAR

SELVAGE   FINISHED EDGE

Figure 1
Partial Blouse Layout

Flowers Galore

DESIGNER
Joyce Baldwin

Top off a pretty floral fabric with coordinated embroidery accents on a detachable collar. To change the bouquet, just make another collar or substitute a flowered scarf.

Design details

The designer started with a standard shirt pattern with collar and collar band. She made slight alterations to the pattern, for the detachable collar. See Figure 1 for details.

Materials and supplies

- Pattern for classic shirt with banded collar
- Fabric of choice
- Coordinating or contrasting fabric for detachable collar
- Interfacing, for collar bands
- Embroidery floss
- Small embroidery hoop
- Notions required by pattern

Construction details

1. Make pattern alterations to collar and band, as indicated in Figure 1.

2. Cut all pattern pieces except collar from shirt fabric, and cut two additional collar band pieces from shirt fabric.

3. Trace collar pattern onto collar fabric; cut a fabric rectangle large enough to fit in embroidery hoop.

4. Complete shirt, according to pattern instructions, but stitch collar band closed as a mandarin collar, instead of attaching to collar.

5. Select embroidery motif from machine stitch options or trace floral motif of shirt fabric. Experiment with placement of motif on collar pattern and, when satisfied, embroider the fabric rectangle by hand or machine, using an embroidery hoop to keep fabric taut.

6. Cut upper collar pattern out of fabric rectangle and stitch to under collar. Attach to additional collar band, to form detachable collar.

7. Attach snaps at matching locations on shirt collar band and band of detachable collar (center back and shoulder seams). Attach snap to tab ends of detachable collar, to hold them together inside the buttoned collar band of the shirt.

Tips from the designer

■ Pretest embroidery floss on a scrap of the fashion fabric and then wash the swatch! It's best to know at the beginning whether colors will bleed or run together. This is worth the extra time whenever you're combining unlike materials in the same garment.

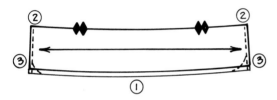

COLLAR

① INCREASE COLLAR WIDTH AT OUTER EDGE GENEROUS 1/16".
② DECREASE COLLAR LENGTH GENEROUS 1/16" AT EACH CF END, TO LEAVE A SLIGHT SPACE BETWEEN COLLAR ENDS AT CF.
③ ROUND SQUARED CORNERS OF COLLAR.
④ ADJUST SEAM ALLOWANCE WIDTHS.

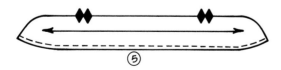

COLLAR BAND

⑤ DECREASE BAND WIDTH AT NECK EDGE 1/8".
⑥ ADJUST SEAM ALLOWANCE WIDTH.

Figure 1
Pattern Alterations for Collar

Plan for the Week

Monday

Tuesday

Wednesday
Pretreat fabrics.

Thursday
Cut out blouse, mark, and interface appropriate pieces; trace collar pattern on selected collar fabric.

Friday
Cut fabric rectangles for detachable upper collar; begin blouse assembly.

Saturday
Complete blouse assembly; embroider upper detachable collar.

Sunday
Assemble detachable collar; make buttonholes and sew on buttons; attach snaps to hold collar in place.

Vintage V-Neck
DESIGNER
Pat Scheible

If you collect antique linens, here's a beautiful way to give them a new life—incorporate them into a modern blouse style, topped off with a touch of hand-crocheted trim.

Materials and supplies

- Pattern for button-front V-neck blouse, or any pattern that fits selected antique yardage
- Handwoven linen toweling
- Hand-crocheted lace edging
- Fine linen handkerchief
- Lightweight fusible interfacing
- Notions required by pattern

Construction details

1. When cutting out the pattern, lay center back and sleeve hem cutting lines along the selvage.

2. Mark buttonhole placement on right front and fuse scraps of lightweight interfacing to the wrong side of each buttonhole.

3. Assemble blouse according to pattern instructions. If the pattern calls for front and neckline facings, omit them. Instead, cut narrow bands from the linen handkerchief and piece as needed to achieve a length equal to the front/neckline edges. Right sides together, stitch the pieced band to the front/neckline edges; press seam toward band; turn and stitch to inside.

4. Make buttonholes and attach your best pearl or horn buttons. Note that the buttonholes are well-supported by the interfacing and handkerchief facing band, and the buttons by the facing band.

5. Attach crocheted lace edging by hand, turning under ¼" (6 mm) at each end. Note that the edging will cover the machine-stitched seamline of the facing band.

Tips from the designer

■ Because the selvages of a handwoven cloth haven't been put under as much tension as a machine-woven, they make perfect already-finished seam edges that also reduce bulk. In the blouse shown here, I pieced the center back seam and the-sleeve hems along the selvages.

■ Handwoven fabrics require, and deserve, some special seam finishes that keep the material from raveling badly, such as flat-felled, French, or Hong Kong. See Figures 1, 2, and 3. These seam treatments are easy to sew once you know how, but it helps to practice on some fabric scraps before stitching your antique cloth.

■ Substituting the lightweight handkerchief band for a full facing is a couture touch—it makes a clean finish on the inside and reduces bulk around the neckline. This works particularly well for linen, which has plenty of body and can support itself without a complete facing.

Plan for the Week

Monday

Tuesday

Wednesday

Thursday
Soak vintage linens, if necessary; pretreat other   fabrics.

Friday
Cut out blouse, mark, and interface appropriate pieces.

Saturday
Assemble blouse.

Sunday
Make buttonholes and sew on buttons; attach crocheted lace edging.

"A little extra thought and careful construction will transform some very fine antique linens into a very fine garment. The heritage linen and crocheted lace in this blouse continue to age beautifully!"

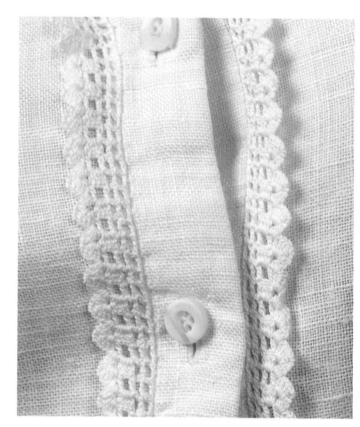

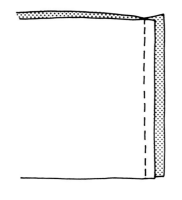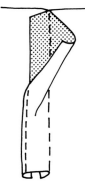

▨ RIGHT SIDE

☐ WRONG SIDE

Figure 1
Flat-felled Seam

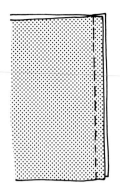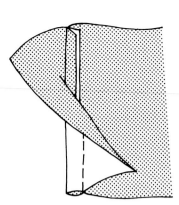

RIGHT SIDE

WRONG SIDE

Figure 2
French Seam

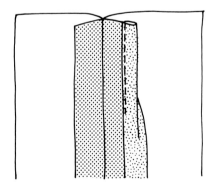

RIGHT SIDE

WRONG SIDE

BIAS STRIP

Figure 3
Hong Kong Finish

HOW TO CLEAN VINTAGE LINENS

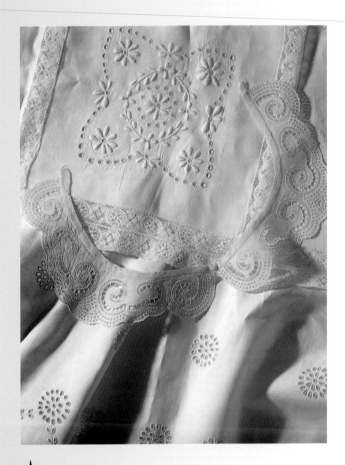

Antique linen fabrics can discolor over the years, but you can safely clean them for a fresh, new appearance. Fill the bathtub or a large basin with tepid water. Add 1 cup of gentle soap flakes (such as Ivory), 1 cup borax, and 1 cup oxygen (dry) bleach. Lay the linens on top of the water and pat gently to submerge. Let soak overnight. Drain the water and repeat at least once more; up to four soakings may be needed. Rinse thoroughly and spread out to dry in the sun. Be gentle when handling the linens; linen fibers are very strong when dry, but quite weak when wet.

Convertible Collars

DESIGNER
Mary S. Parker

This smart-looking weskit blouse features detachable collars so you can get double the wearing mileage with just a little extra work.

Design details

For the two detachable collars shown here, you will cut out the same pattern pieces in the same quantity and follow the same construction steps that you would for a permanently attached collar, with two notable exceptions:

a) Instead of attaching the under collar to the back neckline of the blouse, you will attach it to a separate back neck facing. You will, therefore, cut out a second back neck facing piece.

b) Instead of attaching the under collar to the front neckline and opening of the blouse, you will attach it to separate, shortened front neck facing pieces. You will, therefore, cut out a second set of front neck facing pieces that have been shortened to about 3" (7.5 cm) below where the front edges of the blouse overlap.

Materials and supplies

■ Favorite V-neck blouse pattern

■ Blouse pattern that has a favorite collar style (you will use the collar, back neck facing, and front facing pattern pieces to create the detachable collar)

■ Approximately ½ yard (.5 m) fabric of choice, for each collar

■ Thread to match fabrics

■ Approximately ½ yard (.5 m) lightweight fusible interfacing, for each collar

■ ⅛ yard (.15 m) hook-and-loop tape

■ For pintuck collar: double needle, gimp cord, contrasting thread

■ For entredeux collar: strip of entredeux, zipper foot

■ Notions required by patterns

Construction details

1. Check the "marriage" of the blouse and collar styles by inserting a blouse with the collar you wish to use under a blouse made from your V-neck pattern. The low point of the "V" in the blouse neckline should be low enough so that the selected collar will fasten at the intended point. Check also that the V-neck is not so low that the collar will be too small to fill up the neck area.

2. Assemble the V-neck blouse, according to pattern instructions. NOTE: In some patterns, the collar and upper portion of the front facing are a single piece. (This is true for the wing collar with the gridded pintucking design shown here.) If this is the case for the pattern you are using, simply ignore references to the separate front facing in the following instructions.

3. For both collar versions, fuse interfacing to the wrong sides of the under collar, one of the back neck facing pieces, and two of the shortened front facing pieces.

4. Perform the selected decorative technique on the interfaced upper collar and cut the upper collar pattern out of the embellished fabric. See specific how-to tips below for the different collar styles.

5. Join the embellished upper collar to one of the back neck facings and the first set of front facings (if these are used in your pattern).

6. Join the under collar to the other back neck facing and to the remaining front facings.

7. Sew the upper collar and under collar together along the outside edges, right sides together. Trim seams, turn, and gently press.

8. Use hook-and-loop tape to hold detachable collar in place around the blouse neckline, as follows. Cut the tape into squares. Apply a loop-sided (soft) square to the inside of the blouse neckline at center back; apply a hook-sided (hard) square to the back facing of the detachable under collar at center back. Apply additional sets of squares at the shoulder seams, taking care that the detachable collar will line up smoothly along the blouse neckline and front opening.

9. Mark the front facings of the detachable collar for buttonhole placement, so the collar will be sandwiched between the right and left blouse fronts when buttoned. Make buttonholes and cut open.

10. Try on the blouse and detachable collar, to determine if additional squares of hook-and-loop tape are needed to hold the collar securely in place.

Pintucked collar, on page 90

The design is formed by sewing a grid on the selected fabric with a double needle, prior to cutting out the upper collar pattern. First, sew all the lines in one direction, and then sew the perpendicular lines. Use a width-guiding arm, if your machine has this attachment, or other method to ensure that the lines are exactly the same distance apart. Cut the upper collar from this pintucked fabric.

NOTE: Many sewing machines have a small hole in the needle plate, through which gimp cord can be threaded from below. The cord is then caught in the stitching on the underside of the fabric, and plumps up the pintucked rows, giving them more definition. Refer to your sewing machine owner's manual for details.

Entredeux collar, on page 88

1. Cut two rectangles out of the selected collar fabric that are slightly larger than the upper collar pattern, making sure that one edge is on the straight of grain.

2. With right sides together, align the outside edge of the entredeux with the straight-grain edge of one of the fabric rectangles. Pin in place, with the entredeux on top.

3. Position under the sewing machine needle with aligned straight-grain edge to your right and the bulk of the fabric rectangle to your left. Using a zipper foot, sew the entredeux to the fabric with a straight stitch. Stitch just a thread or two away from the entredeux strip's openwork section. Press seam allowance toward fabric rectangle.

3. Repeat with other fabric rectangle, so entredeux strip makes a dividing line between the two fabric rectangles.

4. Arrange the upper collar pattern piece on the entredeux/fabric piece to find a pleasing placement for the collar. Try to keep the entredeux insertion at least 1½" (4 cm) from the outer edge of the collar pattern.

5. Cut out the upper collar.

Tips from the designer

■ You really get a high payoff from your weekend sewing time if you focus on creating additional detachable collars for a single blouse style. Plus, you get to experiment with new techniques without risking an entire garment.

Plan for the Week

Monday

〜〜〜

Tuesday

〜〜〜

Wednesday

Pretreat fabric; evaluate "marriage" of selected blouse and collar styles.

Thursday

Cut out blouse and collar, mark, and interface appropriate pieces.

Friday

Perform decorative embroidery or technique on upper collar.

Saturday

Assemble blouse.

Sunday

Assemble detachable collar; secure to blouse with hook-and-loop tape; make buttonholes and sew on buttons.

Harlequin Fantasy
DESIGNER
Karen M. Bennett

Defy the ordinary in this colorful blouse with shaped collar, tatted and beaded collar point accents, and a changing palette of buttons.

Materials and supplies

- Pattern for weskit or blouse, preferably one with a generous rounded collar

- Fabric of choice

- 1 yard (.95 m) contrasting or coordinating fabric for collar

- Assorted colors of pearl cotton, size 12

- Frosted glass beads in rainbow colors

- Nylon thread

- Narrow cording, for piping around neckline

- Point turner

- Zipper foot

- Tatting shuttle

- Beading shuttle

- Sturdy paper, such as construction paper or brown grocery bag

- Notions required by pattern

Construction details

1. Trace pattern for triangle point onto sturdy paper and cut out. Label one corner "A," as shown in Figure 1.

2. Place triangle pattern on outer edge of collar pieces, with point A on collar's center front (CF) seam allowance. Trace around triangle along collar edge, repositioning point A next to completed point of previous triangle. See Figure 2. Note that the seam allowance around outside edge of collar is now ¼" (6 mm). See Figure 3. You may have to adjust the width of your triangle pattern, for even distribution between the two ends of your collar pattern.

3. Sew collar pieces together at center front and around outer edge with a very small stitch, following traced lines. Place needle down into fabric at each triangle point, pivot, and continue sewing.

4. Trim seam allowance to ⅛" (3 mm) on edges and around points. Very carefully clip into top of triangle points. See Figure 4.

5. Turn collar to right side, using a point turner for perfect points; press well.

6. Assemble blouse up to collar attachment.

7. For neckline piping, measure length around neck edge of collar. Cut a strip of bias fabric equal to this length and 1¼" (3 cm) wide. Fold bias strip over narrow cording to encase it and sew close to cording with a zipper foot.

8. Baste piping along collar neckline, raw edges even, and turn under ends. Place blouse neckline facing on top of piping and sew facing to blouse with zipper foot, catching piping in between.

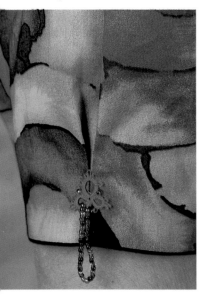

9. To add piping to sleeve bottom, cut off sleeve hem; apply piping as described for neckline, using sleeve measurement and sleeve hem as facing. Stitch underarm seam and tack sleeve facing in place.

10. Shape sleeve hem for beaded accent with a small inverted pleat 1" (2.5 cm) from piped edge; baste to hold in place. See Figure 5.

11. Complete blouse assembly, according to pattern instructions.

12. Sew on different colors of buttons to coordinate with fabric pattern behind buttonhole. Make tatted and beaded accents, and attach with nylon thread to each collar point and top of sleeve pleat.

For tatted clover leaves

Key:

- = picot

+ = join

* = bead

cl = close

R = ring

numbers = # of double stitches

1. Wind tatting shuttle with thread.

2. With beading needle, string 47 beads onto shuttle thread.

3. Tat, as follows:

R1: (2 beads on left-hand thread) 4 * 4 - - - 4 * 4 cl

R2: (1 bead on left-hand thread) 4 + 3 - 3 - - - 3 - 3 * 4 cl

R3: (1 bead on left-hand thread) 4 + 4 - - - 4 * cl

R4: (43 beads on left-hand thread) 2 slide 42 beads up to form large loop 2 cl

4. Tat 13 clover leaves, one for each collar point and sleeve pleat. If desired, tat two more for matching earrings.

For more information about tatting:

Jones, Rebecca. *The Complete Book of Tatting*. London: Dryad Press Ltd., 1985.

Tips from the designer

■ I highly recommend that you make a muslin sample of your blouse pattern's collar first, to test the size of the triangle pattern and to make sure the finished, piped collar will fit the blouse neckline edge. I used three layers of fabric for the collar on the blouse shown here, instead of two; this eliminated having to interface the collar, which would have added bulk to the points.

■ Use a very small stitch length when sewing the collar points, so you can make a sharp pivot at the points. Trim the seam allowances to a mere ⅛" (3 mm) along the triangle edges and across the points.

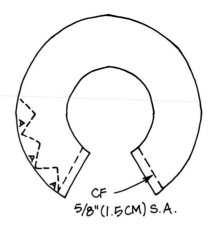

Figure 2

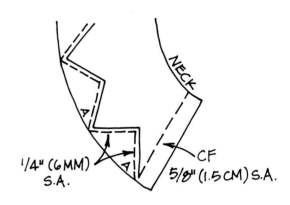

Figure 3

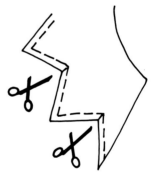

Figure 4

Plan for the Week

Monday

෴෴෴

Tuesday
Pretreat fabrics.

Wednesday
Modify and test collar pattern.

Thursday
Cut out blouse, mark, and interface appropriate pieces; begin blouse assembly.

Friday
Make collar and piping; apply piped collar to neckline.

Saturday
Complete blouse assembly; pipe sleeve hems; make button- holes and sew on buttons.

Sunday
Make and attach tatted clover leaves.

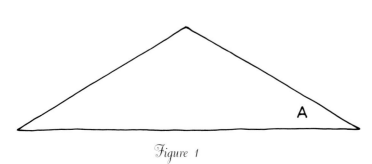

Figure 1

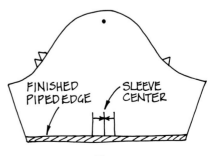

Figure 5

Ethnic Tuxedo Shirt

DESIGNER
Mary S. Parker

Ikat and other ethnic fabrics offer lots of possibilities for creative pleating effects. Why not try a tuxedo-style shirt for a knockout look?

Materials and supplies

■ Pattern for tuxedo-front tunic or big shirt, with tuxedo-style band collar

■ Fabric of choice, plus approximately 1½ yards (1.4 m) extra for sleeve pleating or 3 yards (2.75 m) extra for sleeve and front pleating, if pattern does not feature tuxedo-front

■ Heavy duty spray starch

■ Rayon embroidery thread

■ Bobbin fill thread for use when rayon embroidery thread is in the needle

■ Notions required by pattern

■ Optional pleating device

Construction details

NOTE: You will pleat the fabric before cutting out the pattern.

1. Lay out shirt front pattern on the right side of the ikat fabric, to measure how far in from the edge the pleats should start. Make pleats from this point in toward the center of the fabric. You do not have to pleat the same amount of material as called for in the pattern, because you will fold the pleats marked on the pattern prior to placing the pattern on the fabric. Instead, try to use the fabric's design to suggest how deep the pleats should be and how many you should make (striped fabric is a great help, here).

2. Pin the desired pleats, spray with starch, and iron to set them.

3. Fold the pleats in the front pattern piece and place on the pleated ikat fabric. Cut out one side of the shirt front.

4. Repeat for the other side of the shirt front, remembering to flip the pattern over so you will have a left and a right.

5. Follow the same procedure for each sleeve.

6. Select an appropriate decorative stitch. With rayon embroidery thread in the needle and an appropriate filler thread in the bobbin, stitch the pleats down in parallel rows 4" (10 cm) apart. The final design will be more interesting if you sew the rows at an angle, rather than horizontally.

7. Press the pleats in the reverse direction between your 4" (10 cm) rows of stitching. Stitch again, between the previously sewn lines. You may want to mark the intervening stitching lines with chalk or use a sewing machine attachment to guide you while sewing them. When finished, you will have stitched rows 2" (5 cm) apart.

8. Complete shirt assembly, following pattern instructions.

Tips from the designer

■ It's a good idea to make several pleated and stitched samples, before working on the final shirt. You might need to adjust sewing machine tension, change the angle of stitching, or select a different decorative stitch motif.

■ If you wanted to use just a little pleating, for effect, you could do the back yoke and cuffs instead of the fronts and sleeves of this shirt.

Plan for the Week

Monday

Tuesday

Wednesday
Pretreat fabric.

Thursday
Cut out shirt pieces, except fronts and sleeves; experiment with different pleating arrangements and stitching options.

Friday
Pleat fabric; cut out fronts and sleeves.

Saturday
Stitch pleats with decorative embroidery; begin shirt assembly.

Sunday
Complete shirt assembly; make buttonholes and sew on buttons; hem.

Pintucks for Fun
DESIGNER
Joneen M. Sargent

Take a printed fabric and enhance the design with pintucking. The effect is nicely textured, interesting to look at, and fun to do.

Materials and supplies

- Pattern for tunic or big shirt

- Fabric of choice, plus enough extra for pintucking (see below)

- Notions required by pattern

Tips from the designer

- Try to coordinate the size and spacing of the tucks with the design elements of the fabric, for a neat and balanced effect.

Construction details

1. Cut fabric rectangle(s) measuring twice the width and an extra 1" (2.5 cm) on top and bottom of the pattern piece(s) to be pintucked. On the blouse shown here, the front and back yoke pieces were pintucked.

2. Measure and mark desired spacing of pintucks on fabric rectangle. The tucks on the blouse shown here are spaced ¾" (2 cm) apart, to accommodate the design motifs of the fabric.

3. Carefully fold fabric along pintuck line, wrong sides together, and press. Stitch ¼" (6 mm) from edge of foldline.

4. Press and stitch remaining pintucks, and then press entire piece, being careful not to stretch or distort it.

5. Mark evenly spaced horizontal rows across pintucks. The rows on the blouse shown here are ⅞" (2.2 cm) apart, to accommodate the fabric's design.

6. Topstitch across the rows, reversing the direction of the tucks on every other row. Use a small knitting needle or other aid, to hold the tucks in place while stitching.

7. After all rows are stitched, press entire piece carefully.

8. Cut pattern piece(s) out of pintucked fabric.

9. Assemble garment, according to pattern instructions.

Plan for the Week

Monday

Tuesday

Wednesday
Pretreat fabric.

Thursday
Cut out and mark blouse, except pieces to be tucked.

Friday
Cut fabric rectangles for tucked pieces; measure and mark tucks; begin stitching tucks.

Saturday
Complete pintucks; cut pattern pieces from tucked fabric rectangles; begin blouse assembly.

Sunday
Complete blouse assembly; make buttonholes and sew on buttons; hem.

Embroidered Elegance
DESIGNER
Linda Boyd

Cut the front panels of a blouse into strips and rejoin them with decorative faggoting that is truly elegant. Then, stitch a few rows of machine embroidery with coordinating metallic thread for a luscious shimmer.

Materials and supplies

- Pattern for classic blouse
- Fabric of choice
- Interfacing of choice
- Tear-away stabilizer
- Thread to match fabric
- Metallic thread in coordinating color
- Gimp cord or embroidery floss to match fabric
- Pintuck sewing machine foot
- Edgestitch sewing machine foot
- Notions required by pattern

Construction details

1. Check to make sure you have enough yardage before cutting anything! Cut out all blouse pieces except fronts.

2. Cut two fabric rectangles that are 22-23" (56-58.5 cm) wide and 30" (76 cm) long, and trim away the selvage edges.

3. Using the straight of grain as a guide, cut two strips of fabric from each rectangle that are 2" (5 cm) wide. You will have a total of four strips of fabric, 2" by 30" (5 by 76 cm). These will be the center strips of the blouse fronts.

4. Cut one strip from each fabric rectangle that is 6" by 30" (15 by 76 cm). These will be the center front strips.

5. The remaining fabric rectangles should measure 12" (30.5 cm) wide and 30" (76 cm) long. These will be the side front strips. All of the strips will be reassembled for the blouse fronts.

6. Along each edge of the 2" (5 cm) strips, press under ¼"

(6 mm), and serge or overcast to finish the raw edges.

7. To cord the folded edges of the 2" (5 cm) strips before connecting them with faggoting, refer to your sewing machine owner's manual for details about preferred attachments. (For the blouse shown here, a narrow zigzag stitch was used with the edgestitch sewing machine foot.) Place folded edge of strip against blade of foot, sew two or three stitches, and place needle down in fabric.

8. Lift foot and bring gimp cord or embroidery floss from the right, under the foot, to the needle. Lower the foot.

9. Pull cord up and over the front of the foot and hold it with your right hand against the left of the blade, guiding it as you stitch it to the folded edges of the strips.

10. Cord one edge of each 6" (15 cm) and 12" (30.5 cm) strip, as above.

11. Gently press all corded edges.

12. To join the strips with faggoting, refer to your sewing machine owner's manual for details about preferred attachments. (For the blouse shown here, a honeycomb stitch was used with the pintucking foot.) First, join the 2" (5 cm) strips together with faggoting. Position the two corded edges so they lie in the grooves of the pintucking foot as you stitch. Start about ½" (1.25 cm) from the ends of the corded strips and slow your machine down to half speed, if it has this feature.

13. Apply tear-away stabilizer to wrong side of fabric between faggoted rows. Working on right side, machine embroider between rows with decorative stitch of choice and metallic thread. Tear away stabilizer.

14. Join the 6" (15 cm) strip to one edge of the 2" (5 cm) strips and the 12" (30.5 cm) strip to the other edge. You now have a reassembled fabric rectangle large enough for one blouse front. Repeat for other side with remaining 6" (15 cm)

and 12" (30.5 cm) strips.

15. Cut blouse front pattern from faggoted rectangles, making sure you have a left and a right, and that the strips are symmetrical.

16. Assemble blouse, according to pattern instructions.

Tips from the designer

■ I love the custom look of this faggoting, because it's different from store-bought and I can match it to the fabric of the blouse. However, you can use strips of ready-made faggoting, especially if your fabric is white or black; if your fabric is a color, consider dyeing the white faggoting to match. Even better, practice making your own unique faggoting, using the features of your sewing machine.

Plan for the Week

Monday

Tuesday
Pretreat fabric; experiment with stitching and attachments for cording and faggoting.

Wednesday
Cut fabric rectangles for front strips; cut out remaining pattern pieces, mark, and interface appropriate pieces.

Thursday
Cord edges of strips.

Friday
Attach strips with faggoting.

Saturday
Complete decorative embroidery; cut out blouse fronts; begin blouse assembly.

Sunday
Complete blouse assembly; make buttonholes and sew on buttons.

Ocean Flora
DESIGNER
Karen Swing

Underwater colors and plant forms come to life with fabric dyes on a fluid linen fabric that drapes in a sensuous manner.

Design details

■ The designer made this tunic or big shirt in a white linen, using 100% cotton thread in white. After completing the entire garment, she dyed it with Procion dyes, according to manufacturer's instructions.

■ She then made some simple rubber stamp designs and printed the dyed shirt with a discharge mix of bleach and mona gum powder. The discharge process removes some of the dye in the fabric, as in the lightest blue leaf shapes.

■ She neutralized the shirt with a hydrogen peroxide solution (1 part hydrogen peroxide and 8 parts water), and then washed and dried it.

■ The dark blue swirl and yellow-green squiggle designs were then applied with fabric paint and commercial stamps.

■ She added random embroidered swoops in a running stitch design, with two strands of floss, ending with a single glass seed bead.

■ The buttons were sewn on upside down, to show the flat, plain side.

■ Glass seed beads were then sewn over each hole in the buttons for a luminous final touch. The combination of the buttons and seed beads give a reflective, liquid impression to pull the entire look together.

Tips from the designer

■ I pushed myself beyond my own safety zone with this project, but I learned so much. You can do the same! Take the time to try something new—you will be happy with the results.

Sashiko Sampler

DESIGNER

Mary S. Parker

Put your stitch samples to beautiful use. instead of leaving them in the sewing room. Spotlight your decorative embroidery talents with this gridded vest attached to a blouse in matching fabric.

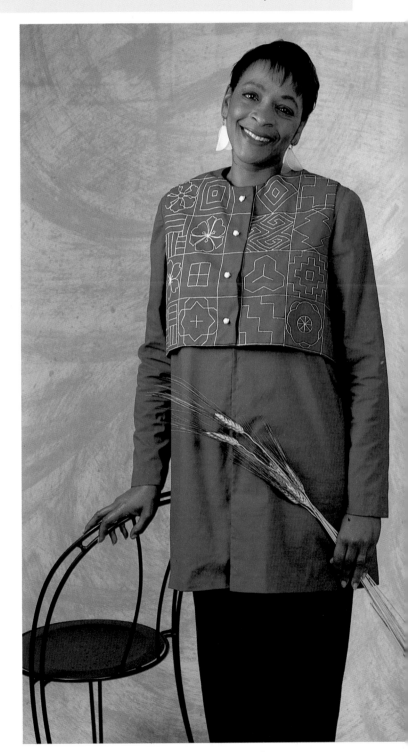

Materials and supplies

- Favorite tunic or big shirt and vest patterns
- Fabric of choice, as required by two patterns
- Fusible interfacing, to reinforce vest fronts and back
- Fusible tear-away stabilizer
- Teflon sheet, usually sold to protect ironing board when fusing interfacing to fashion fabric
- White topstitching weight thread
- White regular weight sewing thread
- Iron-on transfer pens
- Notions required by patterns

Construction details

The designer used a two-step process for making the iron-on transfer pattern for the Sashiko embroidery. The tear-away stabilizer is easier to remove from the fashion fabric after completing the embroidery, if you use a Teflon sheet for ironing the transfer onto the stabilizer before ironing the stabilizer onto the fabric. You can then iron the stabilizer to the fabric at a lower temperature than if you were transferring the design after the stabilizer was attached to the fabric—making it much easier to tear away later.

1. Check that the blouse and vest patterns are compatible in shoulder width and armhole depth. To do this, pin vest front pattern to blouse front pattern, matching shoulder seamlines and center fronts. The blouse pattern should be at least ½" (1.25 cm) wider than the vest front at the shoulder seam. If it is not, choose another vest pattern or narrow the shoulder of the vest. The vest armhole should also be at least ½" (1.25

cm) larger than the blouse armhole all the way around.

2. Cut out vest fronts and back from fashion fabric and selected interfacing. Fuse interfacing to the wrong side of the fashion fabric, following manufacturer's directions.

3. Draw a full-size pattern for your vest design, or adapt a design from a book of shapes and patterns. Photocopy the design and trace over the design lines with the iron-on transfer pens.

4. Place a sheet of stabilizer, shiny side down, on your cutting surface. Place vest front pattern on the upper part of the stabilizer, so the vest shoulders and neck edges are at the top edge of the sheet. Use a pencil to outline the vest front on the stabilizer. Remove pattern, flip over, and repeat this process on the lower part of the stabilizer sheet. You now have both a right front and left front outlined on the stabilizer. Cut out the stabilizer along the two outlines.

5. Lay another sheet of stabilizer, shiny side down, on your cutting surface. Place vest back pattern on the upper part of the sheet, so the shoulders and neck edges are at the top edge. With a pencil, outline the vest back, and cut out of stabilizer sheet.

6. Center the iron-on transfers, ink side down, on top of the stabilizer vest fronts and back that you just cut out, and secure with several pins.

7. Place the stabilizer pieces, shiny side down, on top of a Teflon sheet on your ironing surface. Remove pins and iron the transfer designs to the stabilizer, according to manufacturer's directions. Lift the transfer away and set aside. The stabilizer will lift up easily from the Teflon sheet.

8. With the shiny side of the stabilizer against the wrong side of the interfaced fashion fabric (the transferred designs will be facing up), iron lightly to secure. NOTE: You don't want to bond the stabilizer to the fabric permanently because you will have to tear it away later; iron lightly at first and touch up loosened areas, if needed.

9. Thread sewing machine bobbin with topstitching thread and needle with regular thread. You may have to loosen bobbin tension, as well as tighten needle tension, for a good-looking stitch. Experiment on a fabric scrap before stitching on the garment pieces.

10. The Sashiko embroidery will be stitched with the right side of the fashion fabric against the feed dogs of the sewing

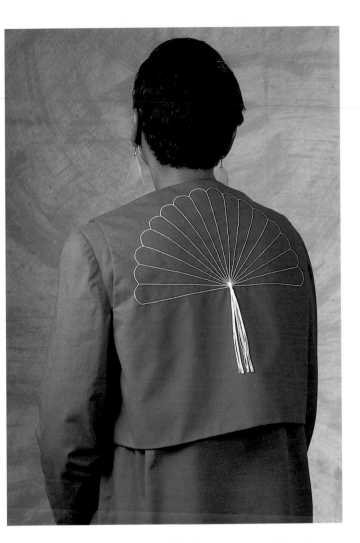

■ I used this grid-front vest to practice many of my favorite Sashiko embroidery designs. You can create your own designs or refer to Sashiko pattern books available at your local sewing store or library.

■ For the fan shape on the back of this vest, I left long thread tails and knotted them together as a fringe, instead of pulling them to the wrong side. The thread tails became an important part of the design.

■ Choose blouse and vest patterns that are simply designed, without a lot of darts, pleats, or other features that might compete with the embroidery. The blouse pattern I used here is a no-collar V-neck style with straight sleeves, and the dartless vest has a high, round neckline.

■ I thought that stitched buttonholes would detract from the clean grid of the Sashiko design, so I substituted hidden snaps for the vest closure and tacked decorative ball buttons on top. No messy buttonholes and the buttons serve as a nice exclamation point to the overall design.

Plan for the Week

Monday

Tuesday
Pretreat fabric.

Wednesday
Modify vest pattern, if necessary; experiment with Sashiko stitching on fabric sample.

Thursday
Cut out vest and blouse, mark, and interface appropriate pieces.

Friday
Cut stabilizer; transfer designs; fuse stabilizer to vest pieces.

Saturday
Complete Sashiko embroidery.

Sunday
Complete blouse and vest assembly; attach decorative buttons.

machine, and the iron-on transfer designs on top. Sew the design, following the iron-on transfer. Stitch the grid lines first, and then sew the designs in each square. To avoid stitching over a loose tail of bobbin thread, always pull the bobbin thread up to the iron-on transfer side (wrong side) of the fabric as soon as you have stitched far enough away that this can be done.

11. When the embroidery stitching is completed, tie off all bobbin threads with their corresponding needle threads in tight square knots. Trim thread tails to about 1" (2.5 cm).

12. Gently tear away the stabilizer.

13. Complete blouse and lined vest, according to pattern instructions.

14. Tack vest to neck edge of blouse at shoulder seams.

Rippling Rings
DESIGNER
Mary Russell

This variation on a traditional patchwork pattern undulates beautifully around and about an easy and flattering blouse style.

Materials and supplies

- Pattern for asymmetrical-front blouse
- Fabric of choice, for blouse
- Assorted fabric scraps, for patchwork
- Invisible nylon thread
- Temporary marking pen
- Notions required by pattern

Tips from the designer

- Don't be afraid to turn a traditional piecework pattern into your own free-form variation. Experiment with placement of the pieced elements until you find a pleasing design. No one will know how many options you looked at before you finally stitched your personal favorite in place.

Construction details

1. Cut out blouse and stitch shoulder seams, according to pattern instructions.

2. Cut arc components out of assorted fabric scraps, following patterns shown here.

3. Piece 10-13 arcs, using 4 center pieces and 2 end pieces for each one.

4. Position arcs on the blouse until you like the arrangement and pin in place. The arcs may be joined together end-to-end in a continuous manner, or joined with a corner square.

5. Mark placement of the arcs on the blouse with the temporary marking pen.

6. Unpin and remove arcs, and join together according to placement on blouse.

7. Appliqué patchwork arcs to blouse, using invisible nylon thread and straight, zigzag, or buttonhole stitch, as desired.

8. Fold narrow bias strips of contrasting fabric and insert under some of the curves, to enhance the pastels.

9. Complete blouse assembly, according to pattern instructions, enclosing bias strips in the neckline and front opening seam.

Plan for the Week

Monday
Pretreat fabrics.

Tuesday
Cut out blouse, mark, and interface appropriate pieces.

Wednesday
Cut out arc components.

Thursday
Piece arcs.

Friday
Arrange arcs on blouse and mark placement.

Saturday
Join arcs and appliqué to blouse.

Sunday
Complete blouse assembly; make buttonholes and sew on buttons; hem.

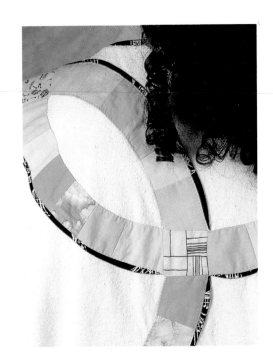

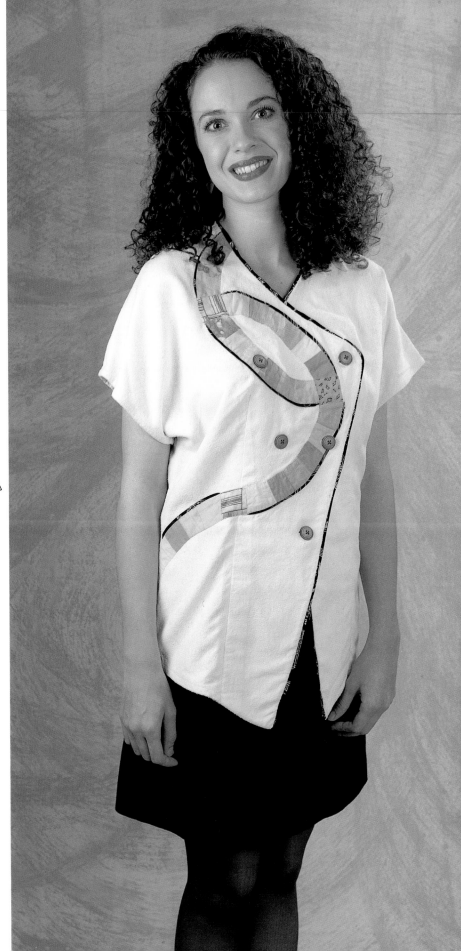

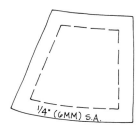 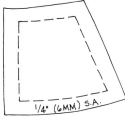

1/4" (6MM) S.A.   1/4" (6MM) S.A.

END PIECES FOR EACH ARC

1/4" (6MM) S.A.

CENTER PIECE
CUT 4 FOR EACH ARC

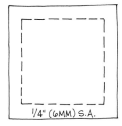

1/4" (6MM) S.A.

CORNER SQUARE
(OPTIONAL)

Eye-Catching Ikat
DESIGNER
Mary S. Parker

Three compatible ikat patterns plus a touch of red add up to a total look that stops admirers in their tracks. They will be impressed with the designer look. and never know how easy it is to put together.

Design details

The designer started with a commercial pattern for a Japanese-inspired blouse. She made no changes or alterations to the pattern, but imaginatively selected complementary prints for the various blouse pieces and then added just enough red to create a designer look. Mixed arrangements of colors and/or prints can be applied to any garment, lending variety and ingenuity to the finished article.

Tips from the designer

There are two ways to measure the amount of fabric you will need when mixing prints and colors in the same project—the "scientific" and the "serendipitous." Choose the method that feels most comfortable:

■ For the scientific method, decide which pattern pieces you want in which fabric. Lay out the pattern pieces for each fabric on a grid-marked cutting board, leaving as little wasted space between them as possible. Remember to stay within the confines of standard fabric widths. Measure the total yardage needed for each fabric.

■ For the serendipitous method, purchase 1½ yards (1.4 m) of each desired fabric. To determine the number of different fabrics you will need, divide the pattern's total yardage requirement by 1.5 and round up. For example, if the pattern calls for 3¾ yards (3.45 m), divide by 1.5 to result in a bit more than 2; rounded up, the result is 3. This means that you should buy three fabrics at 1½ yards (1.4 m) each. With this less-than-scientific method, you will have plenty of fabric left over, which will serendipitously find its way into another sewing project.

Sedona Sunset

DESIGNER
Ann E. Beck

Create an artful blouse like a painter composes a canvas—with interesting shapes, dabs of color, complementary textures, and glowing details. Make it as simple or complex as your taste desires.

Design details

The designer selected a blouse pattern that was already divided into some color block sections. For additional subdivisions, she traced over portions of the original pattern. She then used a different fabric or stitch technique for the various sections and made some custom polymer clay buttons, to create a truly unique garment.

Materials and supplies

■ Pattern for tunic or big shirt, preferably one that is already divided into color block sections

■ Assorted cotton fabrics, including ¾-yard (.7-m) pieces for each sleeve

■ Lightweight fusible interfacing, for collar, cuffs, and placket

■ Fusible tricot interfacing, for strip-woven sections

■ Remnant of fusible web product, for appliqué shapes on placket

■ Teflon pressing cloth

■ Decorative yarns, specialty threads, or embroidery floss in assorted colors

■ Tear-away stabilizer

■ Rayon embroidery thread and/or metallic thread in coordinating colors

■ Rotary cutter, mat, and ruler

■ Pinnable pressing surface and iron

■ Notions required by pattern

Optional tools

■ Open-toe sewing machine foot

■ ¼" (6 mm) piecing foot

■ Pleating device

■ Glass head pins

■ Embroidery sewing machine needle, for rayon thread

■ Metalfil needle, for metallic thread

■ Bodkin

Construction details

1. If you have chosen a pattern that is not divided into color block or piecework sections, you will need to create pattern pieces for each technique. Trace over the original blouse pattern, adding seam allowances, to create the following sections:

■ Left front yoke (weaving)

■ Left front (chevron piecing)

■ Placket (appliqué)

■ Right front (couching)

■ Right side front (flying geese piecing)

■ Back yoke (weaving)

■ Back (free-form piecing)

■ Collar (pleating)

2. Cut out the sleeves from two different colors, being sure to cut one left and one right. Set aside.

3. For the pleated collar, pleat selected fabrics by hand or with a pleating device, varying size and spacing of pleats as

strips vertically over the interfacing in a random or planned pattern, until it is covered. Use a bodkin or safety pin to weave additional fabric strips over and under the pinned strips in a random or uniform pattern. Continue until interfacing is covered, being sure that the strips are close enough together that no interfacing shows through. Place Teflon pressing cloth over the work and fuse the woven strips to the interfacing. Apply tear-away stabilizer to the back of the woven piece. With rayon and/or metallic thread in the needle and all-purpose thread in the bobbin, machine stitch woven piece to embellish and secure strips. Stitch down the middle of each vertical and horizontal strip, in various stitch patterns of your choice and in a random or planned order. Tear away stabilizer.

5. For the strip-woven back yoke, repeat step #4 and add couching, if desired. Place decorative yarns or threads on top of section, and stitch over them with a zigzag or decorative stitch. Use matching or contrasting thread and stitch in a random design or along chalked lines made on the fabric beforehand.

6. For the left front, refer to a quilting book for details about chevron pattern. Create a chevron-pieced section to approximate size of left front pattern piece, and fill in with strip piecing until big enough.

7. For the right side front, refer to a quilting book for details about flying geese pattern. Create a pieced section to approximate size of right side front, and fill in with strip piecing until big enough.

8. For the right front piece, apply decorative threads, as described in step #5 for back yoke.

9. For the cuffs, use Seminole patchwork technique to create a piece large enough for both cuffs.

desired. Preserve the pleats with fusible interfacing on the wrong side. Cut collar pattern out of pleated fabric; cut under collar out of coordinating unpleated fabric. Assemble and interface collar; set aside.

4. For the strip-woven left front yoke, use a rotary cutter and ruler to cut strips of assorted fabrics, in varied or uniform widths, as desired. Finish edges, or leave raw. Using the blouse pattern pieces, cut a left front yoke and back yoke from fusible tricot interfacing. Place front yoke interfacing, fusible side up, onto pinnable pressing surface. Pin fabric

10. For the placket, apply fusible web product to wrong side of fabric selected for appliqué shapes. Cut out shapes, peel off paper backing, and fuse appliqués to placket piece, following manufacturer's instructions. Satin stitch around each appliqué shape with decorative or metallic thread.

11. For back, piece scraps of fabric and leftovers from other sections in a random or preplanned arrangement.

12. Before assembling garment, piece front, yoke, and side front components together to form full front pieces.

13. Create custom buttons from woven strips of polymer clay.

Bake, according to manufacturer's instructions. Glue a shank on the back of each button. Apply gold leaf, according to manufacturer's instructions.

Tips from the designer

■ Selecting many fabrics for a pieced design can be lots of fun for some, but intimidating for others. This blouse could easily be made with a much more limited color palette and then "dressed up" with the decorative stitching.

■ When working with pieced fabrics, choose a garment pattern that is simple to construct, so you can focus on the design techniques rather than the assembly.

■ If you're working with many different colors in the same piece, use grey thread instead of changing colors every few minutes. Grey tends to blend with most fabric colors.

■ Use glass head pins if you want to press a pinned-together section. The glass won't melt.

■ An open-toe embroidery foot for your sewing machine can really help you see what you're doing.

Plan for the Week

Note: pretreat fabric ahead of time.

Monday
Cut out sleeves; pleat and make collar.

Tuesday
Make strip-woven left front yoke and back yoke.

Wednesday
Make chevron left front.

Thursday
Make flying geese right side front.

Friday
Make Seminole patchwork cuffs; appliqué front placket.

Saturday
Piece back; begin blouse assembly.

Sunday
Complete blouse assembly; make buttonholes; hem; make and attach buttons.

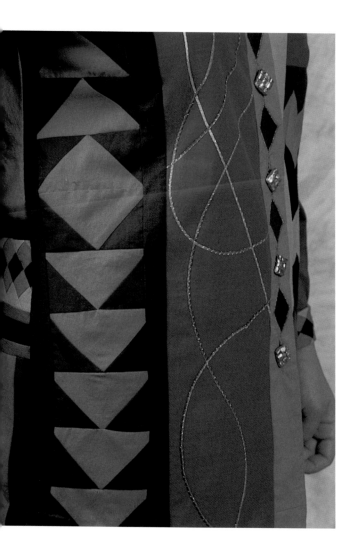

Dogwood Blossoms
DESIGNER
Sherry Masters

The plain overlay of this simple blouse pattern makes a perfect canvas for "painting" with appliqué shapes and hand-embroidered details.

Materials and supplies

■ Pattern for blouse, with front overlay, yoke, or other area that can be embellished

■ Fabric of choice

■ Assorted fabric scraps in desired colors, for branches, leaves, and dogwood blossoms

■ Lightweight fusible interfacing

■ Embroidery thread

■ Fusible web product

■ Tracing wheel and dressmaker's carbon

■ Tracing paper and pencil

■ Freezer paper

■ Fray retardant

■ Wax paper

■ Notions required by pattern

Construction details

1. Cut out all pattern pieces except overlay, yoke, or other area to be appliquéd.

2. Trace the outline of front overlay (or other area to be appliquéd) onto fabric, keeping grain straight. Mark grainline and center front. Fuse interfacing to back of overlay piece, extending 2-3" (5-7.5 cm) beyond the traced outline on all sides.

3. Cut out rough shape of overlay, allowing an extra 2-3" (5-7.5 cm) on all sides for shrinkage during the appliqué process. Set aside.

4. Trace the front overlay pattern piece onto tracing paper, including seam allowances, grain markings, notches, center front, and buttonholes. Make a copy for both right and left sides.

5. Draw your appliqué design onto tracing paper, so you can evaluate how it will look when finished. Draw complete shapes, showing overlapping lines. Extend design lines into the center front and seam allowance areas even if they will be covered up when the blouse is buttoned; this allows a bit of leeway when lining up the pattern during cutting.

6. Next, draw the branches onto paper as individual shapes, counting each branch that forks off a main branch as

a separate piece. All short side branches should be slightly extended, so the ends will disappear under the main branch. These individual drawings will serve as your appliqué pattern pieces.

7. Trace the branch patterns onto the selected fabric and cut them out, keeping track of their placement in the overall design. You may want to number the branches as you draw them and key them to your original drawing. Place on wax paper and apply fray retardant to raw edges; let dry.

8. Pin branches in place on fabric overlay, following original drawing and starting with small side branches. Embroider in place. Continue until all branches are embroidered, making sure the branch that crosses the center front lines up evenly. Complete embroidery on both front overlay pieces before beginning leaves and blossoms.

9. Trace onto freezer paper all leaf and blossom shapes and cut out. With a dry iron on medium heat, fuse the freezer paper leaf patterns to selected fabric. Trace around pattern with fabric marker, peel up freezer paper, and cut out shape. Apply fray retardant to all raw edges, and let dry. Continue to re-fuse the freezer paper to the fabric until all leaf shapes are traced and cut out.

10. Pin leaves in place on fabric overlay, following original drawing, and embroider in place.

11. Repeat process for dogwood blossom shapes and cut from selected fabric. For the three-dimensional effect of some of the blossoms, fuse two shapes together with fusible web and blanket stitch around outside edges, before attaching to blouse front.

12. Sew dogwood blossoms to front overlay pieces with French knots clustered in the center. For the blossoms that will not have three-dimensional effect, sew the petal edges to the overlay with stem stitches.

13. When embroidery is complete, position front overlay pat-

"While I was seeking inspiration for some pink silk I had on hand, I found a postcard from a vacation in San Francisco that had a beautiful arched bridge with dogwood trees in the background. The colors complemented my fabric and I liked the floral theme. My vacation memory quickly became a workable idea for a beautiful blouse."

tern pieces over appliqué design and cut out.

14. Assemble garment, according to pattern instructions.

15. Sew small snaps to the inside of the overlay, to keep appliqué design aligned during wear.

Tips from the designer

■ For the best success with appliqué on garments, choose pattern styles with simple lines and few or no darts or pleats. Also look for large areas to embellish, such as the back yoke, upper side front, or large collar.

■ Choose buttons that will coordinate with your appliqué design, like the leaf-shaped buttons I found for this blouse. These small touches pull the whole look together.

Plan for the Week

Monday
Pretreat fabric.

Tuesday
Cut out blouse, mark, and interface appropriate pieces; cut overlay piece with extra fabric on all sides.

Wednesday
Draw appliqué design.

Thursday
Cut out branches and sew to front overlay piece.

Friday
Cut out leaves and sew to front overlay piece.

Saturday
Make dogwood blossoms and sew to front overlay piece; cut out front overlay; begin blouse assembly.

Sunday
Complete blouse assembly; make buttonholes and sew on buttons and snaps; hem.

Jacquard Bouquet
DESIGNER
M. Luanne Carson

Set off the sleeves from the body of this blouse with decorative double piping for a simple, yet sophisticated design accent. Then, knot some stuffed bias tubes into a belt for a finishing touch.

Materials and supplies

■ Blouse pattern of choice, preferably one that has a bib-type front or raglan sleeves to provide straight side/sleeve seams

■ Fabric of choice, plus additional ⅜ yard (.35 m) each of one companion print and one coordinating solid

■ 2½ yards (2.3 m) cording

■ Hook-and-loop tape

■ Notions required by pattern

Construction details

For double piping:

1. Measure and cut four lengths of cording equal to side/sleeve seams from front underarm, up over shoulder, and down to back underarm.

2. Cut two bias strips of one of the coordinating or contrasting fabrics and cover two of the cording pieces. Repeat with other fabric.

3. Overlay one of the covered cording lengths on the seam allowance of the other and baste together. See Figure 1. Repeat with remaining covered cords. You now have two lengths of double piping.

4. Baste and stitch double piping into side/sleeve seams, using a zipper foot.

For belt:

1. Cut several bias strips of contrasting fabric; stitch, turn, and stuff.

2. Experiment with various knotted arrangements of tubes until you have the desired effect.

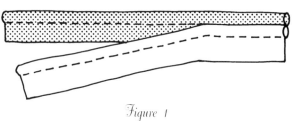

Figure 1

3. When knot is completed, trim ends of tubes evenly so overall length of knotted tubes extends from side waist to side waist.

4. To fill remaining waist measurement, assemble two self-fabric rectangles that will overlap at center back, leaving one short end of each rectangle unstitched.

5. Insert ends of stuffed tubes into open end of rectangle and topstitch to secure tubes.

6. Apply hook-and-loop tape to overlapping belt ends.

Tip from the designer

■ If your double piping is quite fat or wide, you may have to decrease the pattern's side seams a bit, to accommodate the extra width being inserted. Decreasing the pattern can be as simple as increasing the size of the seam allowances on edges where the piping will be applied.

Plan for the Week

Monday

Tuesday
Pretreat fabric.

Wednesday
Cut out blouse, mark, and interface appropriate pieces.

Thursday
Make double piping.

Friday
Begin blouse assembly; stitch double piping into sleeve/side seams.

Saturday
Complete blouse assembly; hem.

Sunday
Make belt.

Tropical Surprise

DESIGNER
M. Luanne Carson

When you need a lift on a grey day, whip up this dazzling splash of color. Then, add some nifty laced tabs that also raise a too-low neckline.

Materials and supplies

- Pattern for basic pullover shell
- Fabric of choice
- Fusible interfacing
- Matching or contrasting decorative thread
- Novelty cord, such as middy braid, soutache, or rattail
- Notions required by pattern

Construction details

1. Assemble blouse according to pattern instructions, up to neckline finishing.

2. Using leftover fabric scraps, make various widths and lengths of interfaced tabs; turn tabs to right side and press flat, with seam to the underside. The widths of the tabs shown here are ⅝" (1.5 cm), ¾" (2 cm), 1¼" (3 cm), and 1⅜" (3.5 cm); lengths are 2" (5 cm), 2½" (6.5 cm), and 3" (7.5 cm).

3. Using matching or contrasting thread, topstitch tabs with decorative machine stitches, as desired.

4. On the wrong side of the blouse, fuse a strip of interfacing around the neckline hole. This will help maintain the garment's shape when the tabs are attached.

5. Fold tabs over, with seam on the inside, and arrange around the neckline, as desired. Baste in position.

6. Secure the tabs and finish raw edges in one operation, by topstitching bias tape to cover the tab ends on the inside.

7. Cut novelty cord and thread through tabs; tack raw ends together and hide within a tab. Tack cord to tabs at center front and back, to hold in place.

Tips from the designer

■ Many times, ingenuity can take the place of pattern alteration. For example, the idea for this neckline treatment came when I needed to do something about a neckline that was too low. By adding these tabs, I didn't have to redraw the pattern for a smaller neck opening. The bonus is ending up with a casual and colorful decorative effect.

Plan for the Week

Monday

Tuesday

Wednesday

Thursday
Pretreat fabric.

Friday
Cut out blouse, mark, and interface appropriate pieces.

Saturday
Assemble blouse.

Sunday
Make and attach tabs; add novelty cord.

Linen Mosaic
DESIGNER
Sherida Ann Stone

Materials and supplies

■ Pattern for basic shell or pullover

■ Fabric of choice

■ Scraps of coordinating or contrasting fabrics, preferably of loose enough weave to fringe easily

■ Notions required by pattern

Construction details

1. Cut out and assemble blouse, according to pattern instructions. The designer replaced the neckline facings with a bias edging, to reduce the bulk of a facing and prevent the facings showing through the light-colored fabric.

2. Cut out squares or other shapes of varying sizes and colors; fringe all sides of each shape to ¼" (6 mm), using a pin to help pull threads.

3. Arrange shapes on the blouse front until you like the look, and pin in place.

4. Using matching or contrasting thread, sew the shapes to the blouse one by one, stitching just inside the fringe line. Unpin overlapping edges and fold out of the way before stitching. Pull all threads to wrong side and tie off.

5. Alternatively, pin the lowest layer of shapes to the blouse and stitch in place; then stitch the next layer of shapes in place, continuing until all shapes are sewn to the blouse.

fringe some "tiles" of coordinating fabrics and place them mosaic-style on the front of a plain shell to make an interesting abstract design. Then, top it off with an unexpected piece of jewelry.

Tips from the designer

■ Feel free to be creative with different shapes, irregular fringing, and wild colors or patterns. Think of the blouse as the canvas on which you "paint" with fabric and thread.

■ When deciding how long to make the fringe, consider the method you'll use to clean the finished garment. Long thread ends might mat together during the agitation of machine washing and drying.

Plan for the Week

Monday

Tuesday

Wednesday

Thursday

Friday
Pretreat fabric.

Saturday
Cut out blouse, mark, and interface appropriate pieces; begin blouse assembly.

Sunday
Complete blouse assembly; cut, fringe, and sew on mosaic shapes.

"Save the Day" Blouse
DESIGNER
Joyce Baldwin

Colorful buttons at the shoulder seam are such a nice detail, you'd never know they mask a neckline measurement error. Creativity can turn any problem into a beautiful opportunity!

Design details

The designer adapted this casual kimono-sleeve blouse from a ready-to-wear model, but the neckline size turned out to be too small to pull over the head and the RTW version was no longer available to examine. Without sufficient fabric to enlarge the neck area and cut a new neckline facing, she salvaged the completed garment with just a few modifications:

■ Remove the facing and open the shoulder seams of the blouse and the facing by 1½" (4 cm), to create a larger neck opening. See Figure 1.

■ Make narrow bias button loops at the corners of the front shoulder seams.

■ Reattach the facing.

■ Sew buttons to corners of back shoulder seams.

Tips from the designer

■ Closures at one or both shoulder seams are a nice alternative, even if you don't have to use them to correct a neckline measurement error. Frog closures could also be used, as well as a jeweled brooch or a scarf threaded through loops all around the neckline. The lesson here is to not panic when something goes wrong; instead, solve the problem creatively.

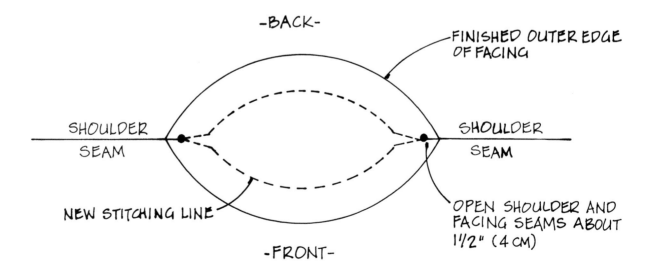

Figure 1

Heirloom Bordello Blouse

DESIGNER

Mary S. Parker

Upgrade a merely serviceable pullover into a truly gorgeous blouse by unexpectedly combining sizzling color with heirloom sewing techniques. This basic short-sleeved pattern will look extra special under a professional jacket, while it shows off your decorative stitching talents.

Materials and supplies

- Favorite pattern for basic shell or pullover
- Fabric of choice
- Tear-away stabilizer
- Decorative thread, for machine embroidery
- Narrow ribbon, if desired
- Wing and double wing sewing machine needles
- Notions as required by pattern

Construction details

1. Cut out blouse front 1" (2.5 cm) larger than pattern piece, around all edges, to accommodate shrinkage caused by heirloom stitching.

2. Cut out stabilizer to same dimensions, and apply lightly to wrong side of blouse front (shiny side of stabilizer against wrong side of fabric). You will be stitching on the right side of the fashion fabric, with the stabilizer against the feed dogs of the sewing machine.

3. Complete decorative embroidery over as much of the blouse front as desired. Use a wide-swing machine stitch to couch over the ribbon, if desired, for the appearance of entredeux.

4. Tear away the stabilizer, after the decorative stitching is complete.

5. Lay pattern pieces over completed fronts and trim excess fabric around edges.

6. Cut out remaining pattern pieces and assemble blouse, according to pattern instructions.

Tips from the designer

- I strongly recommend that you make a practice sampler of your selected fashion fabric, backed with the tear-away stabilizer. Experiment with the wing and double wing needles, which create larger holes in the fabric, and with the various embroidery stitch motifs your sewing machine features. Use a fabric marker to indicate stitch settings and needle choices right on the sampler, so you can see at a glance how you set up the machine.

- Then, use your practice sampler to work out the overall design of the blouse front. This advance planning ensures that the rows of stitching will be symmetrical and the entire design will be balanced and beautiful.

Plan for the Week

Monday

Tuesday

Wednesday

Thursday
Pretreat fabric.

Friday
Cut out blouse front and stabilizer; make a sampler of decorative stitches.

Saturday
Complete decorative stitching on front; cut out remaining pieces.

Sunday
Complete blouse assembly; hem.

Scarf Trick

DESIGNER

Pat Scheible

Transform a pretty one-of-a-kind scarf into a unique blouse. A clever pattern design makes the most of a scarf's limited yardage.

Materials and supplies

- A 38" (96.5 cm) square scarf, for medium size blouse

- T-shirt pattern or ready-made garment that slips easily over the head

- Piping or bias binding to match or contrast, as desired

- Pattern-making or other heavy paper

- Chalk marker

Construction details

1. Trace a neckline from the T-shirt pattern or ready-made garment onto heavy paper. Mark shoulders, center front, and center back. Draw a seam allowance ½" (1.25 cm) inside the neckline shape you traced, and cut out along this line. See Figure 1.

2. Fold down top edge of scarf 12" (30.5 cm), making sure it is aligned perfectly. Mark the lap line, using a straight edge and chalk marker. Cut in 9½" (24 cm) from each side, along the chalk line. See Figure 2.

3. Unfold the scarf, place the neckline pattern in position, chalk around it, and cut out.

4. Fold the 12" (30.5 cm) blouse front back down, right sides together, and sew the underarm seams.

5. Turn blouse right side out. Butt the side panels edge to edge at center front, and fold the front panel back down so the hemmed scarf edge laps over the side panels' raw edges. See Figure 3. Sew a lapped seam, right sides out.

6. Join the side panels, which are butted at center front, with a bridge, lace-attachment, or other joining stitch.

7. Reinforce the point where the body and underarm join with a scrap from the neck opening, if needed.

8. Finish the neck edge with lightweight piping or bias binding, and embellish with braid or trim, as desired.

Tips from the designer

- This simple pattern can be varied so many ways. The two versions shown here illustrate the difference between a fringed and hemmed scarf. Other variations include tapering the sleeves from underarm to elbow; leaving the center seam open or partially open, as in the brown blouse (very nice for summer); shaping the hem by folding up the corners, as in the mottled pattern blouse; adding a drawstring to the waist; defining the shoulders with pads (good for people with sloping shoulders); and making different neckline shapes.

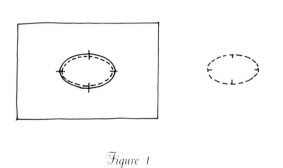

Figure 1

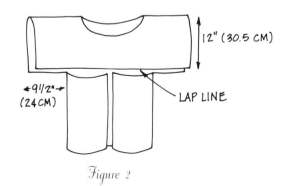

Figure 2

"Scarves don't usually provide enough material for a blouse, but this pattern uses every square inch of precious cloth. It's a variation on the 'Bog Coat,' a garment found on a Bronze Age mummy from a Danish peat bog, and probably is a holdover from the time when clothing was cut from skins."

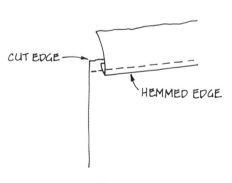

CUT EDGE

HEMMED EDGE

Figure 3

Monday

～～～～

Tuesday

～～～～

Wednesday

～～～～

Thursday

～～～～

Friday
Pretreat scarf, if needed.

Saturday
Trace and mark neckline; begin blouse assembly.

Sunday
Complete blouse assembly; bind neck edge.

Star-Crossed Silk
DESIGNER
Virginia Stevenson

This mock surplice blouse is extremely simple to make. Drape two light-as-air scarves over your shoulders, then shape with a few pleats and secure at the sides, for a dreamy confection of painted silk.

Materials and supplies

■ Two long, narrow dyed or hand-painted silk scarves (or) 1⅞ yards (1.75 m) silk fabric cut in half lengthwise

■ Fabric dye or paint, if using natural silk

■ Thread to match or complement

■ Serger with rolled hem attachment

■ Sewing machine with zigzag stitch

Construction details

1. Trim corners of scarves to form curved edges, for easier serging and to soften the hemline shape.

2. Finish all raw edges of scarves with rolled hem, small zigzag, or overcasting stitch.

3. Drape each scarf over a shoulder; pin 1" (2.5 cm) pleats or tucks in place. Experiment with placement and length of pleats to provide needed fullness at bust, and shape shoulder seams so scarves will stay put. Stitch pleats on wrong side and press toward one side.

4. Sew underarm/side seam to desired length, using a zigzag stitch. Be sure to leave enough of an opening so it will be easy to put on and take off blouse pieces.

5. To wear, put on two pieces separately; insert one arm and the head through the hole. Either piece may be worn on top, to vary the colors or patterns that show in the front.

Tips from the designer

■ This blouse is so versatile. You can wear it backwards, forwards, and even inside out if your serging and zigzag stitches are neat. Each time you wear it, you can vary the colors on top and the interplay between the two pieces.

Graphic Contrast
DESIGNER
Piper Hubbell Robinson

The black-and-white graphic quality of this tunic, combined with comfort fabrics and stylish piped detailing create a knockout look that is cleverly designed to flatter a short figure.

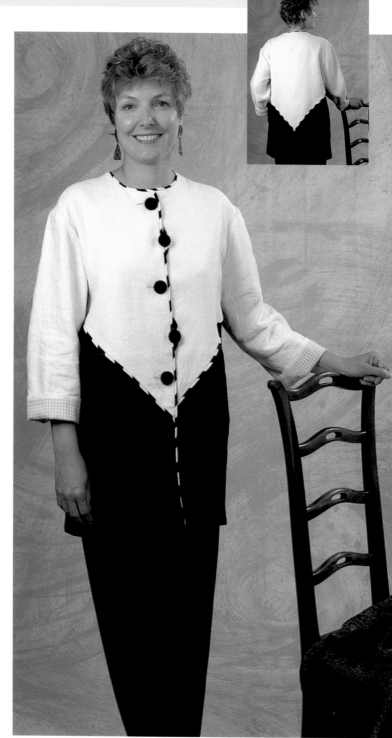

Design details

The designer made this style in a three-quarter length for comfortable wearing with leggings, slim pants, or a slim skirt. However, this length is not always flattering for a short figure, so she split the color arrangement to place black at the lower edge. When worn with black pants or skirt, the overall visual length is increased, the observing eye is drawn up and away from the hemline, and the figure appears taller. She also made these design refinements:

■ The tunic is underlined with a soft and snuggly cotton flannel, for true comfort and a fluid drape to the overall shape. The underlining also hides interior construction, for an impeccably clean finish.

■ A custom piping made from alternating strips of the two fashion fabrics creates an interesting striped accent around the edges and between the color blocks.

■ Pockets are a great convenience, but can clutter up the design lines of the front. Instead, they are sandwiched between the underlining and the fashion fabric, so that no stitching shows on the outside.

■ Button closures are alternated between left and right fronts, with conventional buttonholes and piping loops, for a surprising and innovative final touch.

Cherry Blossom
DESIGNER
M. Luanne Carson

Distinguish the asymmetrical line of a wrap-front blouse with topstitching and a touch of texture. The uncomplicated blouse style and artistic fabric give a classy, painterly impression.

Design details

The designer made this pattern according to instructions, but she dramatized the angled line of the surplice front by inserting polyester fleece between the garment and facing. The fleece serves as a substitute for conventional interfacing, but, more important, it adds a soft three-dimensional quality that is echoed by the two rows of topstitching and the cloud-like fluffiness of the flower shapes.

Materials and supplies

- Pattern for surplice blouse
- Fabric of choice, plus extra for bias strips
- Polyester fleece
- Notions required by pattern

Construction details

1. Cut a strip of polyester fleece as wide and long as the front facing and insert between the two layers during blouse construction.

2. Make a bias band so the finished width is 1" (2.5 cm). Attach it to the front and neckline edges, offsetting it to extend just a little bit beyond the blouse neck edge.

3. Topstitch two rows through all thicknesses, parallel to the inside edge of the bias band. This topstitching secures the fleece and also enhances the relief effect.

Tips from the designer

- If you're going to tuck a blouse in when you wear it, reduce the bulk of a hemline by simply serging or pinking the raw bottom edge. This also eliminates the possibility of the hem's imprint showing through your skirt or slacks.

Plan for the Week

Monday

Tuesday

Wednesday

Thursday
Pretreat fabric.

Friday
Cut out blouse, mark, and interface appropriate pieces.

Saturday
Assemble blouse, inserting fleece strip between front pieces and facings.

Sunday
Make and attach bias band to front and neck edges; topstitch; hem.

"I love this blouse and its quality of softness. The fabric is soft and drapey, the flower design is gentle and spring-like, and the fleecy front edge is so comfy. To me, the whole effect is a study in tranquillity, like an Oriental landscape painting."

Shadow Blouse
DESIGNER
Joneen M. Sargent

A custom lace capelet added to the back of this raglan sleeve blouse makes the garment truly unique, and provides an opportunity to have fun with a fascinating technique.

Materials and supplies

- Pattern for raglan sleeve blouse, or any style that inspires a lace overlay

- Heat-removable stabilizer

- ½" (1.25 cm) silk ribbon

- Packaged lace seam binding

- Assorted decorative threads (rayon, metallic, embroidery, silk ribbon)

- Sewing lubricant, to lubricate metallic thread, if necessary

- Sewing machine needles for embroidery and metallic threads

- Cording and open-toe embroidery sewing machine feet, if available

- ½" (1.25 cm) braid or trim for exposed edges of lace overlay

- Notions required by pattern

Construction details

1. Trace the shape of the overall design or pattern piece on stabilizer with a pencil; this will be your guide to the size and shape of the final lace overlay. Then draw any additional designs, such as flowers, to the interior of the piece.

2. Straight stitch ½" (1.25 cm) silk ribbon directly to the stabilizer at the edges of the traced pattern that will be exposed when the lace is completed (in the blouse shown here, along the cape's lower edge). The silk ribbon will hold the stitching, but remain soft and flexible; it will be covered later with the braid or trim.

3. Straight stitch the packaged lace seam binding to the edges of the traced pattern that will be stitched into garment seams (e.g., shoulder, armhole, neckline).

4. Couch the heavier decorative yarns and threads onto the stabilizer along your traced design lines, using the open-toe embroidery foot, if available, for better visibility. These threads need to be heavier, so the designs won't "disappear" into the background lace. When using ¼" (6 mm) silk ribbon on a design, straight stitching may work better than couching.

5. After all the heaviest design lines are stitched, thread the cording foot with the embroidery thread and couch it in a random pattern throughout the entire piece, using a narrow and short zigzag stitch.

6. After all of the heavier threads are used, begin to construct the background grid pattern that will hold everything in place. Remember that when the stabilizer is removed, the threads will be held in place only by other threads. Therefore, all threads must cross with other threads at small intervals, or large holes will result. Using desired decorative thread, stitch vertical rows ¼" (6 mm) apart, from top to bottom edge of entire piece.

7. With a different decorative thread, if desired, stitch horizontal rows ¼" (6 mm) apart, from side to side of entire piece.

8. When the lace grid is complete, use a metallic thread and appropriate sewing machine needle to stitch a random pattern over the entire piece, to add some sparkle and shine. The lace is now finished.

9. Remove the stabilizer, according to manufacturer's instructions. You may have to repeat the process several times to get all the stabilizer off, or use tweezers to pick off small pieces. Be careful brushing off the heated stabilizer, as the flakes may disperse all over your sewing room.

10. To finish the exposed edges of the lace, stitch the braid or trim on top of the ½" (1.25 cm) silk ribbon.

11. Assemble garment, according to pattern directions.

Tips from the designer

■ Experiment with various decorative and metallic threads, so you will know what effects they create, how to set up the sewing machine, and whether special needles and/or sewing lubricant will be required.

■ Use a sturdy thread, such as a metallic, for the background grid's vertical lines of stitching, to provide strength where the lace will have the most weight and stress.

■ Sewing the continuous up-and-down, back-and-forth lines of the background grid is a perfect chore after a long day at work or a great practice session for a sewing beginner.

■ The heat-removable stabilizer is white and flecks of it may remain in a dark-colored lace, as I discovered. You might want to start with a lighter-colored lace.

Plan for the Week

Monday

Pretreat fabric; trace lace design on stabilizer.

Tuesday

Cut out blouse, mark, and interface appropriate pieces.

Wednesday

Stitch silk ribbon and lace seam binding to edges; begin couched thread designs.

Thursday

Complete couched thread designs; stitch vertical grid lines.

Friday

Stitch horizontal grid lines and metallic random pattern.

Saturday

Remove stabilizer; finish exposed edges of lace; begin blouse assembly.

Sunday

Complete blouse assembly; make buttonholes and sew on buttons; hem.

"This blouse is without a doubt one of the strangest, but most fun, projects I've ever made. I had used this free-form lace technique before, but never on such a broad scale. And now I can envision many other options, such as lace sleeves or a lace scarf to go with a companion garment. The possibilities are endless, the goal is to have fun!"

Confetti Blouse
DESIGNER
M. Luanne Carson

Turn a pair of bright confetti-patterned cottons into a summery outfit. The cool and comfortable blouse goes together in a breeze—just two rectangles connected with small shoulder tabs.

Materials and supplies

■ 2¼ yards (2.1 m) lightweight fabric of choice for blouse

Construction details

1. Cut two rectangles, 27 x 38" (68.5 x 96.5 cm), with the longer measurement on the lengthwise grain.

2. Fold one rectangle in half crosswise, with wrong sides together, to form a 27 x 19" (68.5 x 48.5 cm) rectangle. Fold the other with right sides together. The smaller number is the neck-to-hemline measurement, and the folded edge will be the lower hem. See Figure 1. Lightly press the folded edge to identify the hemline.

3. Open up both rectangles and place them right sides together. Stitch the blouse side seams, beginning and ending 7½" (19 cm) from each end, using ½" (1.25 cm) seam allowances. The unstitched sections will become the armholes. See Figure 2.

4. Turn the stitched tube up along the hemline crease, matching the upper raw edges. You now have a double-layered blouse, with a folded hem at the bottom and open upper edges, which will become the neckline, shoulder, and off-the-shoulder flutters. See Figure 3. Designate a front and a back.

5. To determine the size of the neck opening, indicate the approximate shoulder points on the blouse front and back by marking 6 to 6½" (15 to 16.5 cm) in from the outside corners. See Figure 3. Overlap the front and back at the marks and pin, so you can try the blouse on. Adjust the pins, as needed, to establish a comfortable opening.

6. To shape the neck opening so the garment will sit correctly on the body, you will need to draw a new back neckline and lower the center front. On the blouse front, finish the top raw edges by turning under ⅜" (1 cm) seam allowance and edgestitching; then fold the finished edge under about 3" (7.5 cm). See Figure 4.

7. On the blouse back, draw a subtle shape between the shoulder points or trace the back neckline shape from a commercial pattern. Trim upper back edge along the neckline shape, allowing a ⅜" (1 cm) seam allowance. See Figure 4.

8. Repin the shoulder marks and try on again, checking the comfort of the back neckline shape and the folded-down front edge. Turn under ⅜" (1 cm) seam allowances along the back upper edge and armhole edges, and pin in place.

9. For the shoulder tabs, create two self-fabric tubes 1¼" (3 cm) wide by 1¾" (4.5 cm) long, and press flat. Stitch one end of the tabs to the folded-under front edge at the shoulder

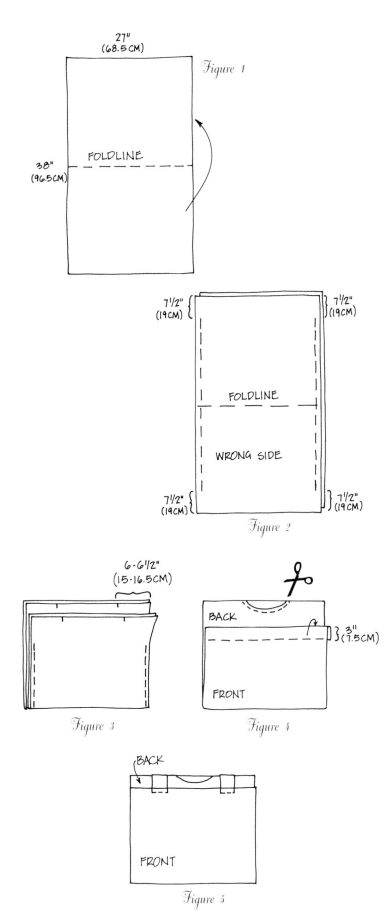

Figure 1

27"
(68.5CM)

FOLDLINE

38"
(96.5CM)

7 1/2"
(19CM)

7 1/2"
(19CM)

FOLDLINE

WRONG SIDE

7 1/2"
(19CM)

7 1/2"
(19CM)

Figure 2

6-6 1/2"
(15-16.5CM)

Figure 3

BACK

FRONT

3"
(7.5CM)

Figure 4

BACK

FRONT

Figure 5

marks. Insert the other end into the pinned back edge, creating an insertion of about ¼" (6 mm) between the front and back. Try blouse on and adjust spacing between front and back until comfortable. See Figure 5.

10. Edgestitch back upper edge and armhole edges, catching tab ends in the seam.

Tips from the designer

■ Because both the back and front are double layers of fabric, the blouse is essentially lined. Therefore, try to choose a lightweight material that won't be too stiff when doubled. This is a great treatment for sheer, summery fabrics!

Plan for the Week

Monday

Tuesday

Wednesday

Thursday

Friday
Pretreat fabric.

Saturday
Cut rectangles; stitch sides and fold up; determine neck opening; finish and fold front edge.

Sunday
Shape back neckline; finish raw edges; make shoulder tabs; stitch tabs in place.

Teal Appeal
DESIGNER
Marion E. Mathews

For easy versatility, change the look of a standard blouse pattern three ways—with pearl buttons, a decorative bow, or a single distinctive button. Use hump-back safety pins, instead of sewing on the buttons, whenever you want to make a quick change.

Design details

The designer started with a standard overblouse pattern, but refined it according to her own tastes and fitting needs:

■ She shortened the blouse by 1¼" (3 cm) and added a bit of flare at the hem by drawing out from the size 14 cutting line to the size 16 on a multi-size pattern.

■ Because she prefers more flare in the blouse body than the sleeve, she narrowed the sleeve a bit, by gradually tapering the cutting line from the notch to the hem.

■ She also took out the shoulder pad allowance, which had the effect of narrowing the shoulder seam and creating a more fitted armhole.

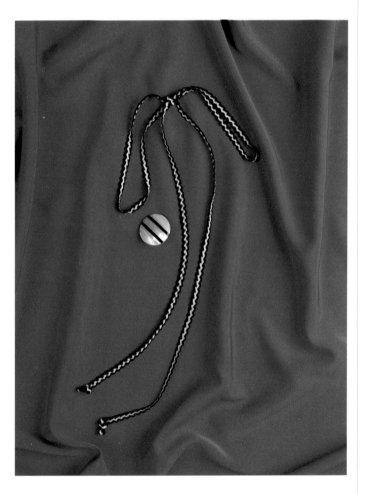

THE DESIGNER ATTACHED THREE PEARL BUTTONS TO THE BLOUSE WITH HUMP-BACKED SAFETY PINS, SO SHE CAN EXCHANGE THEM FOR THIS SINGLE MOTHER-OF-PEARL BUTTON OR BRAID BOW WHENEVER SHE WANTS TO CHOOSE FROM TWO OTHER FINISHING TOUCHES.

Sweet Dreams
DESIGNER:
Sally Hickerson

Design details

■ The designer started with a standard, round-neck tunic or big shirt pattern, but cut it a bit larger, straightened the side seams, and lengthened the overall style for sleeping comfort.

■ She added lace insertions and some corded pintucking to the front and cuff pieces, for a feminine, decorative effect.

■ The cotton lawn fabric makes a super-soft and snuggly garment, and French seams throughout (see page 87 for details) give a finished feel that doesn't irritate bare skin.

■ At the side seam where it meets the curved hem, she appliquéd a small square of the lace trim over the raw edges on the inside. She may be the only one who ever knows about this special lacy accent, but it's a nice touch all the same.

Transform a favorite blouse pattern into a pretty and cozy sleep shirt. A touch of lace and some corded pintucks create a completely different, and dreamy, version of a standard pattern.

Joyce Baldwin

is Assistant Professor of Textiles at Western Carolina University in Cullowhee, North Carolina. She passes on her love of fabrics and fashion design to classrooms full of students, and plans annual student trips to the New York City fashion centers, where she also manages to shop for sewing supplies for her own studio.

Ann E. Beck

is a self-taught fiber artist who has been sewing wearable art for three years, and selling her work at craft shows and by private commissions. She works full time as a CPA for a multinational company and has three small children. She lives in St. Petersburg, Florida, where you will find her sewing in the wee hours of the morning.

Karen M. Bennett

of Alexander, North Carolina, has been a member of the Southern Highland Craft Guild since 1983. An energetic woman, she home schools her four children, keeps a large organic garden, sells her tatting, embroidery, and sewing in galleries and shops, and teaches classes for the local chapter of the Embroiderer's Guild of America. A career highlight was the 1993 commission of a tatted angle for the White House Christmas tree.

Sheila Bennitt

recently relocated to Asheville, North Carolina from Texas, where she sold fanciful fashions from her design studio. She is also a painter and sees many parallels in design and technique between working with fabric and paint.

Linda Boyd

is a walking encyclopedia of sewing expertise and has been a professional dressmaker for many years. She now reserves her sewing time, which she calls her "fun time," for herself and her family. Linda lives in Leicester, North Carolina.

M. Luanne Carson

thrives on the creative process of integrating fabric and style for unusual effect. She combines her formal training in clothing and textiles with her success as an educator to excite her students about their creative potential. Even after 40 years at the machine, sewing continues to galvanize Luanne's thoughts and activities. She lives in Arden, North Carolina.

Laurie Cervantes

has long enjoyed creating wearables and gifts for herself and others. She says that designing and constructing is a very satisfying and creative "workout." Laurie currently enjoys collecting vintage patterns and making them up in new fabrics. She lives in La Jolla, California.

Jean Davidson

is a landscape architect, by profession, and sews for her own pleasure in Aptos, California. She says that sewing has been a common thread throughout her life and she always looks for new new stitching tangents to explore, such as tucking, smocking, quiltmaking, mola appliqué, and weaving. Recently, she has been teaching her granddaughter to sew.

Sally Hickerson

is the hospitable owner of Waechter's Silk Shop in Asheville, North Carolina, a favorite destination for fabric lovers. She also is an expert manager of her time, because she gets a lot of sewing done. Sally is a specialist in customizing patterns for her petite figure and adding flair to everything she makes.

Sonia A. Huber

says that taking classes in pattern drafting, after many years of sewing, opened up a new world for her. She has found that time is short for everyone, so making simple changes to a favorite pattern can take it from the realm of "off the rack" to out of the ordinary.

Lisa Mandle

is the owner and principal designer of Only One, a custom one-of-a-kind clothing and accessories business in Marshall, North Carolina. She has had extensive experience in the fashion and costume design fields, and was selected in 1984 as one of the top ten designers in Washington, D.C. In her current business, she emphasizes the unique qualities of clothing and never makes a design from the collection the same way twice, hence the name, Only One.

Sherry Masters

learned to sew from wonderful teachers, including her mother, grandmothers, and high-school home economics teachers. Her favorite technique is appliqué, but she also enjoys other hand embellishments, precision stitching, and lots of intricate details. Sherry considers herself very lucky to work with other creative people at Grovewood Gallery in Asheville, North Carolina, where she also lives.

Marion E. Mathews

of Asheville, North Carolina, got hooked on sewing when her grandmother let her use the old treadle machine. Since then, she has made her own wedding dress, children's clothes, men's sport coats, and much more. Although Marion soon switched from the treadle machine to a motorized version, she passed on her love of sewing and fabric to her daughter, the author.

Mary S. Parker

is descended from a long line of quilters and seamstresses. Her love of sewing and a fondness for cats have remained constant throughout a changing array of professional career positions. Mary lives in Asheville, North Carolina, and recently moved into a larger house with her understanding husband so that she would have sufficient room for her growing fabric stash.

Piper Hubbell Robinson

operates a one-of-a-kind garment design studio called Wear For Art Thou in Elmhurst, Illinois. She draws on her many years of classical ballet and her formal training in fashion design to interpret line, shape, form, and movement in fabric. Piper says the process of creating garments is completed by the act of wearing them.

Mary Russell

is a quilt artist living in San Luis Obispo, California. Her wearable quilt art has been featured in various fashion shows and publications. She also is the maker of Double Wedding Ring Rulers, which eliminate the need to trace templates when cutting patches for that quilt pattern.

Joneen M. Sargent

likes the creative outlet that sewing provides and loves to try new things. She started sewing back in high school and makes quilts and clothing for herself and her family. Joneen lives in Bristol, Tennessee.

Pat Scheible

is a decorative painter by trade. She designs and creates with fiber, paint, and most any other material that strikes her fancy. Pat lives in Mebane, North Carolina.

Elizabeth Searle

started sewing in the crib, according to her grandmother. She has a dressmaking business in Asheville, North Carolina, teaches creative sewing techniques in area classes, and still has time to experiment with creative art-to-wear clothing for herself and her clients.

Virginia Stevenson

began sewing at the age of three, when her room was also the family sewing room. She taught herself to design doll clothes and was making most of her own clothing by the time she started high school. In 1990, a silk dyeing class she took near her home in Dunedin, Florida awakened a new passion for the interaction of color in wearables and wallhangings.

Sherida Ann Stone

says she has been sewing "forever," at least since she was in an 8th grade Home Economics class. She lives in Weaverville, North Carolina, where she combines her formal design education with a lifelong love of nice fabrics.

Karen Swing

has been sewing since she was 12 years old and is now a full-time fabric artist in Boone, North Carolina. She makes art quilts, but her first love is one-of-a-kind wearables. Karen has been particularly enjoying machine embroidery and experimenting with the different effects of dyeing.

appliqué. Derived from the French word for "apply," a decorative effect achieved by applying different shapes and sizes of fabric to a background cloth.

bateau or boat neck. A collarless neckline opening that is high at center front and back, but extends from side to side in a straight line toward the shoulders.

bobbin fill. A lightweight and very smooth thread for use in the bobbin when stitching with heavier weight decorative thread in the needle. Usually available only in black and white.

broderie. A lace-like trim often inserted in heirloom sewing.

cap sleeve. An extremely short sleeve that appears more as an extension of the shoulder.

convertible collar. A traditional collar with lapel-like revers (see below) that can be buttoned closed at the neckline or worn open.

couching. A method of attaching decorative threads to the surface of a fabric by zigzagging or stitching over them.

dickey. An abbreviated shirt or blouse, designed to be worn underneath another garment, that includes the collar and a portion of the front and back.

dolman sleeve. A sleeve style that is cut in one with the bodice, starting at the hemline and curving out toward the arm.

double needle. A two-in-one sewing machine needle used in machine embroidery and other decorative stitch techniques.

drawn work, drawn thread. The removal of threads from a smooth, evenly woven fabric to create holes that form a decorative effect. Also called hemstitching when embroidery stitches group the remaining threads in different arrangements.

ease. Extra fabric allowed in a pattern to ensure comfortable movement; also called wearing ease. Design ease is added to wearing ease by the style designer to create the desired silhouette; close-fitting styles have less design ease than loose-fitting styles.

edgestitching. Machine stitching made extremely close to a folded edge.

entredeux. Literally, "between two." A decorative or lace-like strip inserted between two fabric panels.

eyelet. A decorative embroidered effect in fabric made by punching small holes and stitching around them. Often used as a decorative edging on yardage. See page 81 for a blouse made from eyelet fabric.

facing. A piece of fabric that is attached to an outside edge of a garment, such as the neckline, armhole, or front opening, to finish raw edges and provide support for added elements (e.g., buttons and buttonholes). Facings are normally sewn on the inside, but can be attached to the right side, as reverse facings, for a decorative effect. A front facing may be cut in one with the bodice or cut separately.

faggoting. Attaching two pieces of fabric, side by side, with decorative embroidery stitches. See blouse on page 98.

flat-felled seam. A method of seam finishing in which one seam allowance is folded over and encloses the other, for a neatened appearance. See illustration on page 86.

French seam. A two-step method of stitching finished seams. See illustration on page 87.

gimp cord. A heavyweight thread stitched into corded buttonholes or pintucks to provide support and definition. See blouse on page 77 for pintucks stitched over gimp cord.

godet. A triangular piece of fabric inserted into a seam that accentuates a flared look. See blouse on page 20.

hemstitching. A decorative machine stitching method that resembles drawn thread work.

honeycomb stitch. A machine embroidery stitch that features an overlapping left-right swing of the needle to create a honeycomb appearance.

Hong Kong seam. A method of seam finishing that binds the raw seam allowance edges with another fabric. See illustration on page 87.

insertion. A method of joining two pieces of fabric with decorative stitches or trims, commonly used in heirloom sewing.

jewel neck. A round collarless neckline shape that is set high and very close in to the neck.

kimono sleeve. Loose-fitting, straight sleeve style that is cut in one with the bodice, as an extension from the shoulder.

mandarin collar. A narrow stand-up collar, derived from traditional Chinese fashions.

marbling, marbleizing. A method of surface design in which fabric is floated in a basin with pigments that are hand-manipulated to create intricate patterns on the cloth.

middy braid. Commercially made, narrow, flat braid that is stitched on top of fabric for a decorative effect.

miter. A method of passing a trim or binding around a corner, to create a flat, square finish. See blouse with mitered braid on page 53.

passementerie. Decorative application of braid, lace, or other trims.

Peter Pan collar. A narrow, flat collar with rounded corners at the front.

pintuck. An extremely narrow tuck (the width of a pin), often sewn in parallel rows for a decorative effect. Pintucks can be stitched over gimp cord, for greater definition. See blouses on page 63 and 77.

piping. A fabric-wrapped cord stitched into seams or other garment features to define style lines or for decorative effect.

placket. An applied band at the front or cuff opening of a shirt. Front plackets can be visible or concealed, as in the blouse on page 73.

point turner. A small accessory with a pointed end, to facilitate turning corners and points right side out.

princess seam. A bodice style that has curved seams from the armhole or shoulder seam, over the bustline, and down to the hemline. Princess garments are flattering to most figures because they are easy to alter for good fit.

pulled thread work. See drawn work.

raglan sleeve. A sleeve style in which the shoulder area and sleeve are cut in one, with underarm seam extending in a straight line to the neckline.

rattail. A shiny, sleek cord used as a trim or decoration.

revers. Pieces of fabric beneath a collar that fold back from the front opening, similar to lapels.

scoop neck. A neckline shape that extends from the shoulder line down the front of the chest in a deep curve.

self-facing. Facing that is cut in one with a pattern piece.

selvage. The tightly woven side edges of yardage.

sleeve cap. The upper area of a sleeve that is eased into the armhole at the shoulder and between the front and back notches.

sloper. A master pattern made to the specific measurements of an individual, used as a template for all garments.

soutache cord. A decorative trim, usually formed from two cords twisted around each other.

sweetheart neck. A shaped front neckline style that curves in toward the center front from the shoulder and down toward the bustline in a modified V-neck.

weskit. Variation of waistcoat. A fitted, short blouse or jacket style. See blouses on pages 55 and 88.

wing needle. Sewing machine needle with flanges or "wings" on each side that pierce the fabric and create small holes for a decorative effect.

yoke. The top part of a garment (shirt, skirt, or pants) from which the remaining fabric hangs. The yoke can be fitted to the body for a flattering effect, while the lower fabric can be draped, pleated, or gathered. A common area for embellishment and decoration.

ACKNOWLEDGMENTS

The behind-the-scenes support system of designers, photographers, models, friends, and others is indispensable to every author. No book would get done without these creative and generous folks, and my sincere thanks go to all of them:

■ the designers, whose creativity, ingenuity, and sewing energy are truly inspiring.

■ the models, who took time away from their real life occupations to dress up for an hour or so, and whose beauty and good humor brought the blouses to life: Dee Ann Allen, Erran Auten, Paige Blomgren, Evans Carter, Jessi Cinque, Rachel Dial, Jennifer Fawkes, Karen Gettinger, Joy Hickerson, Gwendolyn Marvels, Jean McQueen, Celia Naranjo, Micah Pulleyn, Nancy Righi, Michelle Vignault, and Juanita Wright.

■ everyone involved in the photography: Evan Bracken and the professionals at Weststar Photographic and Iris Photographics.

■ the generous folks who lent furniture and accessories to use as photo props: Linda Constable at Sluder Furniture, Ronnie Myers at Magnolia Beauregard's Antiques, Craig Culbertson and Otto Hauser at Stuf Antiques, the staff at Southerlands, and Native Expressions, all of Asheville, North Carolina.

■ Sally Hickerson and the staff at Waechter's Silk Shop in Asheville, who patiently allowed us to use the store as a blouse drop-off and pick-up point and whose passion for sewing is infectious. They also kindly let us turn off the lights and raid their fabric, button and trim inventory for many of the photographs.

■ Lisa Mandle, for her kind-hearted willingness to delay selling her custom-designed blouses so we could photograph them.

■ Dana Irwin, talented art director for the Weekend Sewer's series, fellow lover of textiles, brave model, and owner of an amazing collection of accessories and baubles to put with the blouses.

■ my daughter, Micah Pulleyn, who politely wore many questionable blouse experiments throughout her childhood and who now reminds me to always do something creative with my time.

Index